Where
Leadership
Begins

ALSO AVAILABLE FROM QUALITY PRESS

A Leader's Journey to Quality
Dana Cound

Management Excellence Through Quality
Thomas J. Berry

Integrated Process Management: A Quality Model
Roger Slater

Ethics in Quality
August B. Mundel

Quality Management Benchmark Assessment
J. P. Russell

A Guide to Graphical Problem-Solving Processes
John W. Moran, Richard P. Talbot, and Russell M. Benson

*Benchmarking: The Search for Industry
Best Practices that Lead to Superior Performance*
Robert C. Camp

QFD: A Practitioner's Approach
James L. Bossert

To request a complimentary catalog of publications,
call 800-248-1946.

Where Leadership Begins

Key Skills of Today's Best Managers

Michael J. Langdon

ASQC Quality Press
Milwaukee, Wisconsin

WHERE LEADERSHIP BEGINS:
KEY SKILLS OF TODAY'S BEST MANAGERS

Langdon, Michael J.
    Where leadership begins: key skills of today's best
    managers/
Michael J. Langdon.
        p.   cm.
    Includes index.
    ISBN 0-87389-191-0
    1. Management.   I. Title
HD31.L3156 1993
658.4'092—dc20   92-44801
                                                       CIP

10 9 8 7 6 5 4 3 2 1
ISBN 0-87389-191-0
Acquisitions Editor: Susan Westergard
Production Editor: Annette Wall
Marketing Administrator: Mark Olson
Set in Helvetica Condensed and Cheltenham by
    Montgomery Media, Inc.
Cover design by Montgomery Media, Inc.
Printed and bound by BookCrafters, Inc.

ASQC Mission: To facilitate continuous improvement and
increase customer satisfaction by identifying, communicating and
promoting the use of quality principles, concepts, and technolo-
gies; and thereby be recognized throughout the world as the leading authority on, and champion for, quality.

For a free copy of the ASQC Quality Press Publications
Catalog, including ASQC membership information, call
800-248-1946.

Printed in the United States of America.

  Printed on acid-free recycled paper.

 ASQC
Quality Press
611 East Wisconsin Avenue
Milwaukee, Wisconsin 53202

This book is dedicated to my wife, Jill,

who read it, thought it made a lot of sense,

and urged me to get it published.

Prologue

Thought-Starter

Employees—you, me, and others—with few exceptions, are people who join an organization with an intrinsic desire to at least do a good job; whether it be for personal satisfaction, dedication to the company, or both. The quality of the products or services of these same people working in a group varies from poor to excellent. Barring some strange, pervasive, external influence on the group's environment, the extent to which the group's output varies between these opposite ends of the performance scale *directly and inescapably relates to the quality of their management.*

Contents

Preface

Management was a relatively straightforward matter in the Middle Ages. You inherited the position by virtue of noble birth or by smashing the other contenders and sending them prematurely into the next world. Thereafter, your word was uncontested, and you encouraged its universal acceptance by routine separation of heads and/or other appendages from those unwise enough to protest.

End of Management History 101. We've progressed since then; removal of heads and/or other appendages is no longer socially acceptable and, consequently, the leadership position today obviously requires a more enlightened approach. There is much good news in this respect. More examples of truly enlightened management and the spectacular results it generates are becoming known; yet the practice is spotty, and I continue to observe management time warps where leadership styles are still somewhat in the Dark Ages.

This slightly irreverent treatment of progress in the art of management is leading up to something that you will find as a recurring theme in this book: the position of manager is not one you were born into or have other mysterious rights to. It is a privileged position that you have attained. And while most people are clear about their obligations to higher levels in an organization, this book will, from time to time, put strong emphasis on your relationship with your people—those who work for you—for they allow you the right to be their manager. And you have to earn that right!

I fully expect some to be choking or at least scratching their heads over that last statement. I can only say, keep it in mind, and return to it after you have completed this book—or, better still, after you have practiced its approaches for a while.

A complete set of skills required for successful management is beyond any one book, since the list of such skills would be of almost infinite length corresponding to the wide diversity of occupations. Fortunately, a select few skills apply universally. In this book, I have concentrated on those skills that can be learned and that are proven, time-tested approaches that may be applied to a wide range of situations. In certain cases, I'm giving you a real leg up by adapting some of the methodology currently being used by many companies as they struggle to turn around bad situations brought about by years of mismanagement or, in some cases, by not realizing that the world outside was changing. The leg up I'm giving you is in the fact that these skills, if used now, can head off such declines and the enormous human and financial penalties they exact.

As I was writing this book, I was influenced by a particular travel guide. Like many people, before embarking on a trip to another part of the country, or to a foreign country, I like to plan ahead a little with the help of an appropriate guidebook. Usually, while these books have been adequate in the sense of providing descriptions of hotels, restaurants, and places of interest, they fell short in the sense of guiding. Until one year I bought a guide for a foreign country written basically by one person who had fifteen years' experience in guiding people through this country. The author charted an itinerary that provided a rich experience in itself yet encouraged individual excursions. He described lodgings, restaurants, and attractions in a very down-to-earth manner and made specific recommendations on where to go and what to avoid. He wrote the guide in a very direct me-to-you style that was refreshing in its simplicity and correspondingly understandable. And, while there was only one author, the book encompassed the best thinking of the large number of people the author had worked with. To top off my satisfaction, all this rich collection of information was contained in a book of paperback-novel size and only one-half-inch thick!

And so it goes with this book. I've charted a course for the new or existing manager. I have covered those essentials a manager needs but not constrained anyone from going further in any direction. I have written in a direct me-to-you style because I felt it to be more communicative; I guess that the reason some management books have not fired my imagination has been because of their clinical, detached style, especially in dealing with matters relating to people. In this book you won't find any statistics or graphs relating to people's behavior; I've yet to figure out what I should do having found out in one exercise I was a "triad peak" under "stress conditions." Where I have things to say about people, I will say them and not translate them into a smooth curve.

Again, like the travel guide, although I am one author, I represent the experience of hundreds of people at all levels in whom I have observed the best and the worst in a rich learning experience. And, in case I ever come off in the book as holier than thou, let me add here that its content is also enriched by experience gained from a healthy portfolio of personal mistakes. Thus, you can avoid making such mistakes—and have time to make some new ones of your own!

I would like to acknowledge the help and encouragement of Gene Behun, former Xerox manager, who read through an early manuscript, strongly endorsed it, and encouraged me to get it published—then admitted that he had taken on the task with great apprehension about how he would be able to handle his friend (me) if it was bad!

Introduction

One of my key objectives in writing this book was to have people say this about it: "If you only have time to read one book on management, make it this one." Another key objective was to write it in such a way as to keep the readers' interest. It may be the first management book that, in the parlance of literary critics, is "impossible to put down." Most of all, I wanted it to meet the needs of a wide range of managers: those just starting to those who have been managing for some time yet are less than satisfied that they are achieving the twin objectives of motivating their people and serving the best interests of the greater organization. And that thought leads to a third objective: self-fulfillment for the manager and his or her people.

The book's small physical size is no accident. It's in keeping with my intention of holding the readers' interest. It's not one of those books that numb the mind with exhaustive detail, often based on a single theme. Instead, it's crammed with a very comprehensive range of information vital to the enlightened manager; information that is normally only amassed by reference to several books or by attending a series of courses that stretch over a period of time often too long to satisfy immediate needs.

Very early on in the book you will find a chapter called "The Oasis." Reading this chapter may well be one of the most important things you do in support of your career as a manager. It deals with something that profoundly affects your future ability to be a truly successful leader of people —your ability to develop an effective environment. It includes a questionnaire that will enable you to evaluate your present performance on this extremely important aspect of management and that clearly indicates the kind of conditions and values that must be present for such an environment to exist. Few will be able to ignore the profound messages in this chapter, and you can practice its teachings immediately upon putting down the book. Indeed, I am confident that most managers will behave differently at the very next encounter with one of their people!

Following chapters draw you gradually into a process during which you will take stock of where you are relative to others and determine how you might start out if you are a new manager or an existing manager heading up a new group. Chapters 5 and 6 deal with a customer concept that may surprise you. This topic continues to be of extreme interest to companies that are attempting to turn around a losing trend. You will see how to apply what they are learning in a proactive sense rather than as a belated rescue operation. The remaining chapters deal with the most essential skills a manager needs: skills such as making decisions, running meetings, planning, solving problems, interviewing, administering performance appraisals, and providing sensible levels of documentation. Particularly in the area of decision making, you may be pleasantly surprised to find a level of simplicity and pragmatism that actually encourages use of these skills. Too often, this process is made to appear highly complex, and consequently, just plain overwhelming.

1

Authority

Let's get this topic out of the way fast, because the word *authority* barely belongs in a present-day discussion of management. I'm not talking here about authority in the sense of being able to sign for expenses or grant a leave of absence; I'm talking about the use of authority as a means to get a group of people to do something. The more fashionable word today might be *autocracy;* sounds nicer, but it's similar. Webster defines *authority* as "the power or right to give commands, enforce obedience, take action, or make final decisions." Well, that makes things pretty clear, doesn't it? Or does it?

Many years ago, I was in a management course when one of the other students asked a question in which he used the term *authority.* The instructor suddenly became quite agitated. "Authority?" he said, "authority? The only authority you have is that which your people allow you to have!" He didn't go on to explain his outburst but seemed to dismiss the question with contempt.

Despite his seemingly incensed reaction to the question, I have often reflected on the truth of his statement. And I have often observed the results of managers who rule from a position of authority. The results inevitably follow this model:

Authoritative Management Style	→	Initial Good Results	→	Mediocre Results	→	Anarchy

Yes, one can initially obtain good, even outstanding, results with the use of authority. And one can probably sustain these good results (for example, high output) for some considerable time. But, inevitably, stage two comes: mediocre results. The reason for this should not be a mystery. The sustained use of authority as a means to derive a certain level of performance from a group of people will eventually lead to resentment of that authority and, worst of all, will suppress the minds, the sense of involvement, the ideas, and the natural talents of the people working in this mode. Consciously or subconsciously, those minds, those talents, are turned off from contributing to the success of the enterprise. Such a loss inexorably leads to the mediocrity stage of my model—mediocrity not necessarily in comparison with another area in the same organization, but certainly in comparison with another group of people favored with a more enlightened form of management.

Now to the last stage of the model—anarchy! You're probably thinking "Anarchy? That's a bit strong, isn't it? And what do you mean by anarchy anyway?" In answer to the last of these questions, anarchy in the workplace is something that may occur after a prolonged period of working under the authoritative style of management that initially led to mediocrity. And, in true "Catch 22" style, it is more likely to occur when a manager misguidedly intensifies this authoritative style in order to improve the inferior performance it has already caused. Consciously or subconsciously, the minds of the people being managed in this way will be turned away from contributing to the success of the enterprise. In extreme cases, they may apply their talents toward "fixing" the management or organization responsible for their unhappy state. Hence, a form of anarchy develops: perhaps a strike, perhaps an overthrow of the upper echelon of management. It's true that things don't often reach that stage, but it's not necessarily the worst thing to happen either; it's not clear to me that endless mediocrity is better than anarchy, which might at least clear out the mess and lead to starting over with a more enlightened approach.

To further clarify what I'm getting at, let's go back to the model in its entirety and think about where it might apply. Let's start on a grand scale and think about events in the late 1980s and early 1990s in eastern Europe. Historians will write thousands of pages to document what happened, but at the risk of seeming a bit cavalier, I don't think they would quibble with my application of the model as a very simple illustration of the key stages in socioeconomic breakdown in those countries; that is, very authoritative style of government leading to initial good results (one might question: how good?) followed by mediocre economic results and social decline; ultimately followed by anarchy.

Alright, if that was a bit too global for some, let's bring it closer to home. Let's not think about the relatively rare cases of anarchy but the much more prevalent condition of the model: the authoritative management style. Can you not think of a group that is showing signs of strain from such a style? How about the nursing profession? Certainly they're not paid well enough for the responsibility they undertake—particularly in some of the higher-stress areas such as the operating rooms and intensive care units. But, if you listen to what they are saying, their concerns do not just result from low salaries. In many instances, they'll tell you that what they need is a sense of mutual respect between them, their management, and other higher-level professionals. They'll also tell you that they wish to feel like partners in the enterprise, not just an expendable resource being deployed in sufficient quantities to cover the needs as perceived by their management.

The enlightened manager realizes that he or she does not have some inborn right to exert authority over others in order to get things done. Rather, this manager realizes that a manager's position is a privileged one and that a person has to earn the right to that position—not just from higher levels of management but also from those whom he or she manages. It is this latter aspect that I hope to get across in this chapter.

In summary, when authority is used as the means to motivate people, a weakness will eventually manifest itself in some form. Authority is a crutch used where real management skills are lacking.

If you are already managing, pause for a while before moving on and think about your own style. How much of what your group does is dictated by your rules or rules you hand down from above? In contrast, how much does your group do as a result of their involvement in designing the work approach? If the proportion of the former is large, you may have a problem building.

2

The Oasis

This chapter is about something that profoundly affects the level of your success in applying all the other teachings in this book. This something is so important that, without attention to it, you are unlikely to obtain the level of group performance you aspire to. Moreover, this something is probably the single most important aspect affecting the ability of a group of people to compete successfully with another group, whether that other group is down the street or halfway around the world. Finally, this something is very often neglected as large organizations focus on structural and management changes in efforts to improve the bottom line, yet if properly cared for, it will improve that bottom line—not just in the near future but for the long term.

This *something* is, quite simply, the environment you create for your people. The environment will so strongly bear on your effectiveness in managing a group of people that it will bring lasting benefit to both them and the organization. You cannot implement any of the skills taught in the remainder of this book to maximum effect unless you do so in a positive, constructive environment. And while you can always look to people in your group for expertise in a variety of purely task-related matters, they quite rightly look to you to set the tone of the environment. It is clearly up to you. Even if the environment of the larger organization is not ideal, you almost always have the opportunity to reach for the ideal within your group. Hence, the title of this chapter—"The Oasis."

Clearly this chapter is very much about you, and we will return to you in a short while. But first, let's get a little deeper into this topic by looking at two management traits that are often in evidence where the environment is poor. These are perhaps two of the most damaging traits I have observed in the management scene. They are *egotism* and *complacency.*

Let's take egotism first. You have probably seen the type of managers I'm thinking of here. They are highly motivated in directions that lead to personal gratification and career advancement, but they appear to place much lower priority on the well-being of their people and even, sometimes, on the company. They are very results oriented, especially as indicated by the bottom line. They often move methodically from one position to another in accordance with their own personal career path plan or, sometimes, in order to be long gone when a downturn occurs. They are, to put it politely, politically astute, and they are not to be confused with the truly healthy, ambitious people who achieve similar goals while exercising fairness with their people, with people at all levels, and with their organization. Their people may do quite well generally, but this happens incidentally rather than as a result of an intentional effort to make it thus.

Bad? Not entirely. As implied, the people who work for these kinds of managers may well benefit from the momentum they create, even if it is mainly directed toward their own personal gain. However, there are some truly bad players in this category: those whose personal ambitions, often accompanied by a dictatorial style, lead them to riding roughshod over their people. Such people leave a trail of casualties behind them: very often the best kinds of people, the kinds of people that an organization cannot afford to lose, but to whom such behavior is odious. In a way similar to that discussed in chapter 1, these people can deliver results for quite a long time, but the weakening of the organization (which surely takes place under such methods) will eventually show up on the famous bottom line, by which time a major human-resource-reconstruction effort will be needed. Again, I'm not suggesting that focusing on personal gain necessarily results in bad management; indeed, by merging personal ambition with concern for people, a truly outstanding manager can evolve.

My reference to the bottom line in the previous paragraph brings an incident to mind. At one company, in a routine operations meeting, the vice president observed that the performance ratings for the employees were not meeting a standard statistical distribution (that is, the distribution of rankings 1 through 5, with 1 being poor, 5 being outstanding). Thus, he demanded that his managers reclassify their people in order to yield the requisite number of 1s and 5s. This attempt to force people to fit a statistical distribution had serious consequences at all levels (and let's here acknowledge that the "bush-telegraph" inexorably penetrates the security of higher-level meetings and broadcasts very efficiently just about any news likely to affect the welfare of the population it serves).

While the point was not entirely without validity, the dictate for adherence to an arbitrary distribution was hideous. Clearly it affected the morale of the lower-rated people, who knew all too well that a move to a 1 rating, even if accompanied by a get-well plan, was also a move in the direction of the door. But it just as seriously affected the morale of most of the managers, who were faced with carrying out an order that violated their own sense of fairness and that crudely overrode their own judgments based on their intimate knowledge of the people concerned. This is the kind of thing that can happen when people are thought of only as numbers.

Now, let's look at complacency, because I think this is where the greater problem lies. First, I had better define what I mean by complacency.

Complacency is—

— feeling that everything is going along reasonably well and not asking the question "what could be improved?"

— assuming that if the job is getting done, everything is okay.

— not occasionally asking oneself whether the group's output is what the customer wants.

— not feeling the need to take the time and trouble to be in touch with the feelings of the people in the group.

— being vaguely aware that one or more of the group has been unhappy for an extended period and just hoping things will work out.

— not identifying with the people in the group in such

a way as to take an interest and pride in their achievements—and to stand up for them within the larger organization.

— being aware of power plays within the group by individuals or cliques, yet not sensing the detriment to the performance of others and, therefore, of the group in total.

These descriptions admittedly stretch the meaning of complacency a bit; perhaps the word *neglect* also applies. The real point is that being a manager requires constant attention to such matters. Even the term *being a manager* bothers me slightly because it suggests an achieved state, an arrival, where in fact it should be regarded as a position requiring sustained and dedicated effort to maintain and improve the overall quality and achievement level of the group—more of a journey than an arrival.

As already implied, and sad as it may seem, the group headed by the egotist may be better off overall because the egotist will at least generate more action, from which more opportunity will fall out—notwithstanding the fact that the personal casualties are likely to be more spectacular also.

However, neither of these preceding styles is likely to produce the healthy and positive conditions needed to encourage and sustain superior performance by a group of people. So let's explore some of the workplace conditions that are associated with sustained superior performance. We'll do it via an exercise in which the focus is on you and your relationship with your people. If you aren't currently managing a group, don't skip the exercise; the content should be just as meaningful to you. You might even want to approach to it from the point of view of how you feel your manager should respond to it.

Following is a series of statements that bear upon group environment. Your job is to choose the response to each statement that most accurately describes the state of affairs in your group. There are no catches intended, and your intuition will almost certainly tell you where I'm heading. Think about each statement for a few seconds and then circle the appropriate response. Be as totally objective as possible with your responses (a polite way of saying no cheating, no fudging, no hedging). And do relax. After all, you're doing the grading! The scoring system works as follows:

5 Absolutely true

4 Generally true

3   Somewhat true

2 Well, sort of

1 Hmm...

Note: In the questionnaire the term *group* can describe a number of structures: for example, your *group* may include more than one level. While I can't cover all possibilities, following are some variations of groups:

Project manager with 10 people reporting.
Group = 10

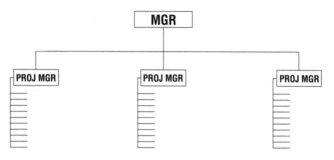

Manager with 3 project managers, each with 10 people
Group = 33

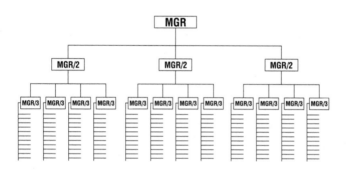

Manager with three next-level managers, each of
whom has 4 project leaders.
Group = 15

Now, the statements:

1 You know for certain that each individual in your group knows exactly what you expect of (a) the group and (b) each individual.

5   4   3   2   1

2 You know for certain that each individual in your group is equally challenged relative to his or her intrinsic capability.

5   4   3   2   1

3 No member of your group would be reluctant to come to you with a problem out of fear that to do so would lower his or her standing in your eyes.

5   4   3   2   1

4 You have met with each individual one-on-one at least once within the last six months to discuss career growth, likes or dislikes about the job, and whatever other topics each individual brought into the meeting at your invitation.

5   4   3   2   1

5 You visited every individual in your group casually at his or her workplace over the course of the last five to ten working days. (In the event your people are geographically far removed, change "five to ten days" to read "as often as necessary to maintain personal rapport and ensure that each person knows they matter to you.")

5   4   3   2   1

6 During the past six months, you and your group have gone off site for a fun event such as a picnic or luncheon, where the emphasis is on the social side, with business secondary or nonexistent.

    5   4   3   2   1

7 During the last four weeks, you have held at least one meeting with your whole group to let them know how the group is doing compared with its objectives and, if your group is part of a larger organization, how the larger organization is doing.

    5   4   3   2   1

8 You know of at least one outside interest (hobbies, sports, and so on) for each member of your group who has been with you for more than a few weeks.

    5   4   3   2   1

9 When you run across a member of your group, perhaps in a hallway, you warmly exchange smiles and greetings.

    5   4   3   2   1

10 You are receiving suggestions for improvement in group operation from at least 50 percent of your people over the course of a year, and you join with each suggestor in evaluating the idea with a view to possible implementation.

    5   4   3   2   1

11 Your people participate in setting objectives and making plans to achieve them. If you were suddenly called away for a month, there would be no shortfall in progress toward these objectives as a result of your absence.

5   4   3   2   1

12 If your best friend's son, daughter, sister, or brother were to start work in your group, you would not feel a need to excuse (to your best friend) any aspect of the group's performance and general morale that is within your realm of responsibility— your oasis.

5   4   3   2   1

End of statements. I'm not going to ask you to add the numbers, because I don't think a numerical sum is necessarily very meaningful in such a subjective exercise. You have probably arrived at some constructive thoughts and conclusions already, just by the nature of the questions; and I have to assume that you would only skip a question if it were absolutely inappropriate for you due to extraordinary circumstances. Suffice then to make the following observations on your scores:

— All 5s or mostly 5s: You are a gem, and I'll bet that you have a strong, highly productive, and competitive team. I'll also bet that a very high degree of mutual respect exists between you and the team and between team members.

— Mostly 4s and one or two 3s: You are on the right track and are doing many things right. But you will need to push yourself harder in the areas of low scores if you want a team like the one described in the preceding paragraph.

— All 3s: That's average, and you'll probably get average results. It may be adequate, but is *adequate* all you want?

— Many 2s and 1s: Oops! Work to be done. The big question is whether you embrace the importance of the environment at all. If you do, then a review of the statements and your responses should give you some clues as to where to begin overhauling your management style. If you don't presently believe it's worth the trouble to develop a positive environment, but nevertheless envy the success of enterprises that consistently demonstrate superior performance, at least take the trouble to evaluate how the leaders of these enterprises would fare given the preceding statements; I'm confident that in most cases you would see relatively high scores. I would also strongly recommend you read *In Search of Excellence* by Thomas Peters, published by Warner. It's been around a while, and I'm only sorry that the important message in this book has escaped you thus far.

Some of my own research into the benefits of a positive environment has been quite unintended. For instance, I often visited the plants of companies who were making something for my project. In many cases, these were sterile walk-throughs that, without persistent questioning from me, did not provide much insight into the nature of the operation. However, there were many that did, and I remember one company in particular. There, the workers were extremely industrious and it was clearly not a charade for visitors. Moreover, along with being industrious, the people were cheerful. Even if busyness can be faked, it is almost impossible to fake a workplace full of cheerful people. If I stopped to look at the work of one individual, the supervisor would introduce that person, describe his or her task, often mention more personal attributes, and then back away with confidence as that person related, with considerable enthusiasm and pride, his or her part in the company's work on my project. When I mentioned my observations to the supervisor, I saw the same enthusiasm and pride as he explained to me how everyone was involved in the planning of the work, how workers received a bonus at the end of any month in which they collectively exceeded plan, how they got together for social events, and so on. While the bonus was undoubtedly an incentive, the most important aspect of this operation was that the environment had been created and nurtured so that everyone had a personal stake in the enterprise—and felt good about it!

Closer to home, I was fortunate enough to spend many years in the company of managers who, for the most part, strived as I did to achieve a positive, supportive environment for their people. With few exceptions, the sustained high-quality team and individual performances occurred in the domains of those enlightened managers and their people. I frequently found, as did these other managers, that someone moving to my group from a group where the environment—to put it politely—did not have a high priority would first need a period of adjustment and would then go on to greatly improved levels of personal performance and group contribution. At times, we seemed to be in the rehabilitation business.

Take the case of Arthur (not his real name) who was "made available" to me during a period when people were scarce. His availability was largely due to a recent history of lackluster performance. I talked with his current manager, somebody I knew and respected, and found out that Arthur had only recently been passed on to him. His feelings were that Arthur had talent but that something about his previous management did not bring out the best in him.

Within a few months of joining my group, Arthur established himself as a major force on a team that improved a performance attribute of an existing product by a factor of four. Within eighteen months he was promoted. While I certainly tailored my initial approach to Arthur based on the history he came with, it was clearly the environment that my people and I had collectively created, together with his own intrinsic talents, that allowed Arthur to realize his full potential. You see, I was only with him a small fraction of the time; but the environment was always there.

Your own plan for cultivating or improving your group environment will be strongly suggested by the previous exercise, in which you scored yourself relative to twelve key statements. In most cases, the statements directly indicate the desired actions or behavior, so your scores should define your priorities.

To gain more objectivity in dealing with a relatively large organization, you might provide the set of statements to your people and have them score you. Of course, the wording will require slight modification. I have been on the receiving end of such a survey and found it to be extremely helpful. If you do something like this, arrange it so that your respondents are assured anonymity, thus enabling frankness of responses. For the same reason, such a survey should not be initiated with fewer than three people. If you do have such a small group, you might just as well sit down and discuss the statements openly—which is perfectly okay and consistent with the air of trust you need to generate for such an undertaking.

Those who are just moving into a new management position—and who, therefore, felt that none of the statements in the exercise applied to them—should nevertheless study them carefully; consider them as key objectives for the environment you will create in the coming months. I don't suggest that anyone adopt all the implied objectives to the letter; do, however, consider each statement as you tailor your actions to your own circumstances.

———

At this point, I must introduce a caveat. In the exercise you went through, you no doubt detected considerable emphasis on a theme of caring for people. The caveat is that you must not confuse this theme with the style of management variously referred to as laissez-faire, country club, or anything-for-peace, in which the manager typically avoids confronting any issues or pursuing any actions that could create conflict with one or more members of the group. Such a style approximately fits the category of complacency and neglect that I covered in the discussion of damaging management traits at the beginning of this chapter.

———

Once you have decided on a course of action to improve your workplace environment, you will need to turn your attention to the key factor in successfully carrying out your intentions. That key factor is your people's perception of you. The next few pages are intended to encourage you to do some very deep thinking about yourself.

Notice that I used the expression "your people's perception of you." I'm probably going to cause some controversy here, but I'm going to state that your people's perception of you is something you have to work on; in other words, you can't always act exactly as you feel. There will always be times when things are not going well for you and it is only natural that you will have your down days. That's OK. What isn't OK is when your irritation (or for that matter, your elation on up days) begins to color your judgments and your dealings with people. That's when your own red-alert system needs to go off and remind you of your role relative to the people you manage. If they understand your problem, they might be able to rationalize and tolerate your irritation. Yet it may only take one unexplained mood swing to lead to apprehension and distrust on their part, thus impairing your effectiveness in creating a positive environment.

In continuing to explore the aspect of how your people perceive you, you will need to flip roles for a while (that is, to think about what you would like to see in someone whose position relates to you in the same way that your position relates to your people). Think of a person you know or once knew to whom you would feel comfortable talking very frankly and openly; a person to whom you felt you could turn for advice, for help in solving a problem, for input when reviewing how to go about a project, and so on. Maybe this person is, or was, a respected teacher, a doctor, or a good friend—maybe even the salesperson who helped you make a good selection or the boss who listened to your admission of an error and not only didn't castigate you but set about helping you to correct the error and by so doing, got the very best out of you. Think about this person, and especially think about your lasting impressions of him or her.

What made this person approachable in the first place? What mini-environment did he or she create that made you, your endeavors, your concerns feel supported? What was it that made you feel you didn't need to hold back, that you could trust this person to be fair with you,

that you could review all the pertinent facts without embar-
rassment? Pause a few moments to think.

What qualities did you come up with? Many of you
may have only recalled one or two predominant impressions. Especially in someone whose professional reputa-
tion you did not know previously, your impressions may
only include a smile, a warmth of manner, friendliness without insincere gushing. For someone you knew better, your
impressions probably also include characteristics such as
competence and experience in a field similar to yours.

Now let's see if we can summarize all the characteristics this person might have possessed. Perhaps they were
the following:

Competence

Experience

Fair-mindedness

Trustworthiness

Interest in you and your circumstances

Approachability

––––––

If you successfully flipped roles a few pages back, you
can flip back now, and I'll continue under the assumption
that you have found at least one person in your memory
who fits the mold. Now, how do you measure up to this
person? But first, why should you want to? Hopefully, you
already answered that question in your own mind when
you searched for this example of a person who took the
trouble to understand your situation and joined with you in
seeking the most positive and constructive course. If this
person left this kind of impression on you, why shouldn't
you consider his or her behavior as your model? But now

our interest must focus less on the person and more on the six attributes.

These attributes are key to a manager's ability to create the right kind of environment for each individual within his or her group and, thus, the group as a whole. So it is important that you critically review yourself against each one. While you may be able to assess your own competence and experience, you may find it more difficult to see where you stand with regard to the other four attributes. In fact, you may need someone close to you to help with the evaluation—someone fair-minded, trustworthy, interested, and approachable!! I can't do this for you via a book, though I will be discussing approachability at some length later in this chapter. Perhaps the person you thought of in the exercise you just went through is the person to assist you in this task. While we're at it, I'll try to guess the person you chose as your exemplary individual. I would not be surprised to find that the person falls into one of the following categories:

A parent or close relative

A family doctor

A family lawyer

A religious leader

An outstanding manager (of course!)

Notice that a sense of family runs through this list—except maybe the last on the list. Actually, the outstanding manager of people *does* develop a concept of family in which he or she is the head. Some may find this a little too rich and would prefer the term *team*—rightfully very popular these days as we struggle to understand the enduring and productive people relationships. I prefer the term *family* because I see a better analogy; whereas a team tends to suggest (to me anyway) a group of people with relatively similar strengths and capabilities, a family suggests a greater variety of these attributes. Is that important? Absolutely!

Like a family, your group is likely to have people of widely varying strengths and talents—especially if it is a group you have inherited rather than selected one by one. And, as in a family, you must give each person ample individual attention while preserving the overall integrity and level of accomplishment of the whole. This means that, in your one-on-one interactions with your people, you approach them according to their individual strengths. In your group, just as in a family, you are likely to have people who are brilliant, people who are less brilliant but very persevering, people who resent structure, people who are slow, people with serious personal problems, people who lack confidence, and so on. You cannot expect optimum results by applying a broad-brush style of management to a work group any more than you can by applying that kind of approach to a family.

If you work for a large company, you may by this time be thinking that this striving for the ideal environment may be all very well in theory, but how can you make a difference when you are surrounded by people who don't have the same set of values? Well, I can tell you from personal experience and from observing many other managers that you can always create your own oasis. And even if the movement doesn't spread, the respect of your people and your own self-respect will reward you. Chances are that the results will show and that the movement will spread. Note, however, that the oasis concept does not mean siding with your people against "them up there." That is absolutely unacceptable and ultimately disastrous for everyone! The oasis concept means setting acceptable standards for you and yours within the framework of the larger organization. If there's something wrong with that framework, that is something you must try to correct at the appropriate levels. If you join a movement against "them up there," you become one of a rebel group, with the result that you will soon lose the group's respect and, ultimately, your own self-respect; and the group will have lost a leader.

Now, as mentioned earlier, I'm going to return to the attribute of approachability. I hope that I have already partially conveyed a sense of what this means. In large part, of course, approachability results from a sense of trust you build up over the long term. But one aspect of it is more immediate, and it has to do with the impression you give. Be very self-critical here: Do you give an impression that encourages people to come to you with things they deem important, things they would like to discuss? Do you feel you encourage that kind of disclosure in the same way as that favorite person you thought of in the little exercise above?

Let's get quite personal. Take a look in the mirror: Do you see someone you would go to with a serious professional problem and discuss it nondefensively? Or do you see something more stern in your expression, something perhaps similar to a previously known, forbidding authority figure in your life?

Let me confess that I have a particular body language problem here: when I am deep in thought, or even relaxed and not actually laughing or smiling, I have a rather stern, forbidding look about me. I don't know if I was born that way or whether I cultivated it, but based on sight alone, I would hesitate to approach the person I see in my shaving mirror in the morning. Fortunately, people close to me helped me understand it; also, I was able to do something about it. No, I didn't get a face-lift! All I did was smile more and generally lighten up when dealing with people. I can assure you the results for me were very positive, and I only wish I had been aware of this aspect much sooner; and not only as it pertained to the workplace.

I'm talking here about the same old problem that can come up in a job interview: the first few seconds are crucial. So critique your approachability quotient (everyone's heard of *I.Q.* now I want you to remember the importance of *A.Q.!*). If you see the need, lighten up! You may need to smile more when you encounter someone (by the way, smiles are infectious—you'll see!), or act in a way that puts the other person at ease. Lighten your verbal approach a bit too; instead of "What's the status of the Wilkinson account?" try "How goes our battle with the Wilkinson account?" If you wear glasses, make sure they are not the kind that make you look formidable—unless for some reason you feel the need to. If you're not sure what you need, ask your spouse or a good friend. This does not mean you have to act out a character that isn't you. It does mean you may have to work on your A.Q. to ensure you get the best out of any encounter.

The good news about improving your A.Q. is in the results. I can guarantee you that attention to seemingly trivial details such as just mentioned will reward you very soon and very substantially. Go ahead, start tomorrow. Heck, start now! Don't overdo it, though, or people will think you've flipped; but work it into your daily life, and you will be rewarded to an extent that may surprise you. And when you've got that underway, start thinking of other ways to improve your A.Q.!

Now, how do you know when you've got your environment headed in the right direction? Well, as I've previously stated, it's a never-ending process of improvement, so let me answer that question by saying you are well on the way when—

— your people come to you before you have to go to them when something is going wrong, and they discuss the problem and their involvement without reservation.

— your people come to you with suggestions for improvement, and you don't feel threatened.

— your people come to you to discuss the personal problems they feel may affect their performance, and you have realized that it is practical to keep a box of tissues on hand.

— one of your people brings you up to date on their tennis or culinary achievements because you have shown an interest in this other aspect of their being.

— one of your people makes a presentation to a group, and you are hanging between apprehension and pride.

———

That brings us to the end of this chapter. It's probably the most difficult chapter in the book because it deals with a seemingly intangible aspect of management—the workplace environment. I have tried to make the subject more tangible by illustrating the kinds of conditions and values that make or break an effective environment, and you have completed an exercise that should have given you a clear sense of specific actions you can take. I have also guided you into thinking about how your people's perception of you can affect your ability to successfully carry out these actions—from which, you should be able to see what changes you might make.

The chapters that follow will benefit anyone seeking to develop new skills or revitalize old ones; but however much you benefit from your reading from here on, you will gain infinitely more if you open yourself to the message in this chapter. Specifically, begin to develop your own plan for providing an environment in which you and your people can build increasingly higher levels of professional success and personal achievement.

3

Taking Stock of
Your Personal Situation

The chances are you fall into one of the following categories:

1 You are going to be a manager, and your organization is sending you to a training course.

2 You have just become a manager, and your organization has set you up for a management course in six months' time. Based on experience and observations over a considerable period, I know that many of you will fall into this category.

3 You are already managing and would like to know if you've got it about right.

4 You are comfortable with a totally autocratic style and don't need any further insight into the job. In

this case, you probably choked on the chapters about authority and the oasis, and it's surprising you have reached this page.

5 You are already a very good manager but don't yet know it because nobody has told you and because you thought you couldn't be one unless you spent years taking management courses.

6 You did take management courses for years and have come to realize that people just don't seem to relate to all the neat theories that made so much sense at the time, moreover, your people all seem to be behaving like individuals!

7 You have been diligent, studied this theory and that theory, and are thoroughly confused because theories seem to come and go like fashions.

8 You are an experienced manager, and you have just been appointed to head up a new group; in addition to being new to the group, you have no previous experience in the kind of work they do.

What to do?

I have to assume that you made the correct decision in seeking or accepting a management position—whether recently or way back when. I have to assume the following as well: you really wanted the opportunity to lead a group of people, you are prepared to correctly judge and deploy the human and financial resources required to get the job done, you understand that those who put you in this position expect you to continuously improve the level of achievement of the people you will manage, you understand you will have to balance your major responsibility for the success of the larger organization with your equally major responsibility to offer opportunities for personal fulfillment to the people in your group, you understand that lack of success in another part of the larger organization or a general economic slowdown might make it difficult for you to provide the kind of compensation and opportunity you would like to accord your people, you understand in good times or bad you are required to compare the individuals in your group and make clear distinctions regarding the level of financial reward and advancement opportunities to be accorded, and you understand that so much of what you achieve will depend on your effectiveness in working with people.

A bit heavy going? That's good, because if you were able to just breeze through that lot, there's something missing. And I admit that I sneaked it in to stimulate you to think about whether you are cut out for management. The preceding paragraph is woefully incomplete but, from it, I hope you got the sense that management involves a number of potentially stressful aspects. You don't have to feel comfortable with all aspects, but if, for example, you have a low tolerance for stress and a low tolerance for people, you might not be right in a management position; at the very least, you have considerable work to do on yourself.

Let's touch a little more on the subject of stress. *All* jobs involve stress. Airline pilots, assembly-line workers, building contractors, janitors, teachers, refuse collectors, salesclerks, surgeons—all these jobs are potentially stressful. And one should not assume that an assembly-line worker is any less stressed than a surgeon; repetitive tasks can be highly stressful. The stress that the conscientious manager experiences stems largely from the dual, and sometimes conflicting, responsibilities of doing what is best for the whole organization and providing the opportunity for self-

fulfillment and personal growth of a diverse group of individuals.

Now, I'm not a psychologist, and I'm not going to try to
give you some way to determine how much stress you can
or should tolerate. But I'm not going to leave you hanging
either. This book is going to help you reduce stress in two
areas.

The first area for stress reduction derives from my
strong emphasis on the way in which you should relate to
the people you manage. You can be assured that this
theme will be continued throughout the book, and I want
you to be assured that the more contact you make with
your people, the less stress you will feel about this aspect
of your job. I have frequently seen office-bound managers
increase contact with their people through informal meetings or, better still, by informally wandering around the
workplace to chat with them. The correspondingly
increased comfort level in these managers, in their rapport
with their people, in overall morale has been quite evi-
dent—sometimes dramatically so; and I didn't learn this
solely by watching others!

The second key area for stress reduction relates to
your competence. As you read this book and build your
management skills, you will also increase your confidence
and comfort level in dealing with those who look to you for
guidance.

I remember one year returning from my vacation and
sitting down with the person I had left acting in my place.
He seemed to have aged visibly in my absence. I asked him
how things had gone, and he blurted out, "!###**!!!!, I had no
idea how much crap you kept off our backs." Yes, he had
found the job stressful and he had also come to realize two
important things: (1) it hadn't been as immediately satisfying as he had expected and (2) a large part of a manager's

job, especially in large, heavily bureaucratic companies, *is* to keep certain things off people's backs so they can get the job done. The happy news is that he continued to pursue opportunities for management, and I really believe he will do well—*because* he was thinking deeply enough about it to feel the particular stresses and doubts that come with this job. And if you have doubts as to whether you can be a successful manager, I would say go ahead. Do it! To have some doubt means you have thought about it seriously, and that alone puts you ahead.

What are these "certain things" that a manager keeps off people's backs? You'll read about a lot of them later, but some of them can be covered at this point in the book. "Certain things" are notoriously more prevalent in larger organizations, where the communication task is proportionately more time-consuming. I know! It shouldn't be that way! And that's a nut that needs cracking, too; but let's accept that larger organizations always tend to require more of these "things." These "things" include verbal presentations and paperwork.

Let's take verbal presentations first—the kind where you need to communicate technical status and budget matters, for example, to peers and higher-level management. I firmly believe in doing most of the work for such presentations myself. First of all, I am practiced at it and, therefore, can do it faster than most of my people. Secondly, I consider it necessary for a manager to know his or her people's work well enough to be able to describe it fluently in any presentation. I make one exception to this rule, and that is when one of my people stands to benefit from the exposure afforded by personally presenting their work (but more on this in the chapter on performance appraisal).

Paperwork! Again, a large organization thinks it needs lots of it, and in the long run, you might want to work on proposals for reducing it. But initially, your job is to mini-mize the pain it causes your people.

This reminds me of an incident. Once, one of my people came to me and complained about the length of time it took for a work order to reach the model shop after I had signed it. The two of us looked into it and found that after leaving me, the order went to our area's controller, who then sent it to another building where someone in procurement verified the dollar level of my signature, authorized the order, and returned it to the controller, who knew my signature authority anyway. To cut a long story short, we had a rub-ber stamp made for our controller's clerk, who used it (plus her initials) to authorize the order, thus saving almost one whole week. Of course, the rubber stamp took a while to obtain; you see, the order for it went to the other building for signature verification and...!

There are numerous examples such as this one, where it is the manager's duty to remove or alleviate obstacles to progress that inevitably result from any paperwork system. For instance, my secretary had a kind of credit card for use in a company store. My people would frequently borrow it in order to obtain things quickly. Fortunately, computers are not intelligent, otherwise the one in the store might have begun wondering what my secretary would be doing in one month with three calculators, seven Phillips screw-drivers, and eighteen AA batteries!

Note that I am not advocating cheating the system. Much better to help change the system to better serve the people it is supposed to serve. In the case of the rubber stamp, we did just that. In the case of the credit card, our mutual trust allowed us to operate in this manner.

One more example, and then we'll get back to work:

At a company I worked for, an employee-involvement group made up mostly of secretaries undertook to study the suspected excessive cost of buying supplies from the company's in-house stationery store. One of the items they fell upon was a charge of ten dollars for one thousand paper clips. A quick survey of prices at places such as drugstores indicated they should cost around one dollar and thirty cents. Investigation revealed two key points: (1) the in-house store stocked paper clips only in boxes of one hundred and (2) their cash-register program was such that any entry less than a dollar was automatically registered as one dollar. Thus, a request for one thousand paper clips resulted in ten boxes, each of which registered at one dollar...!

Just before we go back to work, let me say that I find that last example very satisfying in many ways. It provided us an inexpensive opportunity to marvel once again at our own infallibility. It also demonstrated the power of a group of dedicated employees who challenge a problem—regardless of the amount of money involved. Finally, particularly because the problem was solved, it gave us something to smile at, and as you go through this book, I hope you will sense that I don't believe life at work has to be without its lighter moments. In fact, in my experience, shared expressions of humor in the workplace (not the personally malicious kind) have tended to coincide with high levels of energy and morale.

In summary, there is a wide variety in levels of management training. Furthermore, there is not a direct correlation between good managers and the amount of training received (but that's not an excuse for not taking some management-training courses; you certainly should). In addition, a particular kind of stress comes of dealing more with people, systems, and events than with things. And, if you have just *some* doubts, I'd say "Go for it!" You are ahead by thinking enough about your position to feel that way; besides, if you don't go for it, you'll always wonder what might have been—and that can be stressful! Finally, the manager's job can be stressful if done well, because much of the time it involves battling with organizational "things" that threaten the productivity of your people.

A special word to people who have been appointed to a position but who have little or no experience in the kind of work carried on by the people in the new group. You will have a problem due to this lack of experience only if you don't handle things properly. If you do handle things properly, this could be one of the best things that ever happened to you and the group. What to do? Don't try to bluff your way through; your new group is much too smart to be taken in. Be open about it from day one, and immediately set about learning all there is to know. Respect and self-respect will follow.

In a large company I worked for, a vice president of engineering was announced. It was made clear that he had virtually no experience in engineering, having come directly from field operations. He went about the new job rather as suggested above; since this book didn't exist then, I believe he simply followed his natural common-sense approach to things in general. To cut the story short, he went on to be a well-respected, outstanding leader—one of the very best to hold this position. So, if you are just entering a similar situation, take heart. The people who put you there have probably seen qualities in you that more than offset a temporary lack of background.

4

Getting Started

Reading hint: As with all chapters in this book, the intent is to reach managers at all stages of maturity—from new managers to seasoned veterans. If the title or opening words of any chapter appear to relate to those less experienced than you, it is strongly recommended that you still read that chapter. By the act of buying the book, you have shown an interest in improving your performance, and even if you only discover one fundamental thing that you haven't been doing or find one thought that inspires you to reexamine your current practices, your time will have been extremely well spent.

If you are a new manager, you've probably inherited a group of people and a task all at the same time. Or, you may have been handed a task and now have an opportunity to form a group from scratch. Either way, your first job is to figure out just what the task is all about; and if you have inherited a group, you'd better figure it out fast, even if you have to stay up nights to do it.

How do you do this? Talk to the person who appointed you, to the previous manager, and to the people who are the customers for what you do. (I'll talk more about *customers* later.) Put it all together only to the extent that you have a fair idea of what's expected. Then have your first meeting with your people, knowing that you can demonstrate some grasp of the group's responsibilities and that this will be a positive factor in their initial acceptance of you. (Uh-oh, I can just imagine the authoritarian choking again: "Whadya mean *acceptance?"*) You need to have this meeting as soon as possible. (Note: If a substructure of leaders already exists, meet first with them; this is just common courtesy.)

Don't try to do too much at this first meeting. I suggest you kick off by introducing yourself and giving a little background about yourself, your work experience, and some personal things such as your hobbies. In the personal area, be light and lively to help break the ice; but if you are not good at jokes, don't try!

Now, if the group is not too large, go around the room and ask each person to describe his or her role in the group as well as something more personal; it seems to work quite well to ask each person to describe a favorite thing. You will probably be pleasantly surprised at how the whole group loosens up in response. But be open about why you are doing this. If you don't explain, people may see it as a trick, and it won't work. Say something like this: "I don't want this first meeting to be too stuffy, and I would like to begin knowing something about your interests other than your jobs." And mean it!

While still in this meeting, set the stage for the next one. Its purpose will be to jointly discover what the group's task is and to begin developing a strategy for approaching that task. Especially if you are taking over an existing group, plan to have a one-on-one meeting with each person quite soon. Remember, your arrival on the scene, presumably replacing someone the group was used to, feels like a significant upheaval and adds a new element of uncertainty in their lives; they will certainly be wanting to know how it is going to affect them personally. Holding one-to-one meetings shows your sensitivity to their feelings. If you plan to do this, though, say so.

Now, take care of any administrative-type announcements, and ask if people have any questions. If they don't, close the meeting. If they do have questions, avoid the temptation to wing the answer because you want to prove you know what you are doing; there's a very good chance you'll make yourself look silly. Instead, take down the question and return later with a well-considered answer.

The next meeting is crucial, for here you will start to develop an understanding of the group's objectives. Moreover, you will do it *jointly* with those who have the experience to contribute to that understanding and who are, after all, the people who bear most of the burden of achieving the objectives.

Let's pause here for a moment, because I expect some of you are thinking that this is rather risky right at the outset—that it's nice but too democratic.

Winston Churchill once said something to the effect that democracy is a poor form of government but that the only thing worse is the alternative. The same applies here. Certainly it can be scary, and certainly, I didn't always do it in the past. But if you look around at what's going on in many companies today as they scramble to recover their competitive edge, you'll see just such efforts: groups getting together in democratic fashion, at all levels, to revisit what their job really is and how best to do it. Unfortunately, doing it belatedly like this often means that things had degenerated badly (for example, loss of market for a product, low morale, poor relationships between management and other staff, and so on) before they realized the need.

The opportunity is there for you to be proactive and do, in partnership with your people, what these companies are now doing too late: establishing or reestablishing focus on the true task and the ultimate objective—customer satisfaction.

The next two chapters deal extensively with what this means and what it requires. Obviously, this discussion is for everyone—not just new managers.

5

The Customer Concept

OK. Per the last chapter, you've introduced yourself, you didn't get eaten, and you have realized that your new group is just as apprehensive about the future as you are. What next?

Well, next is to set the foundation for what you and your group are going to do in the future. The basic premise is that we all have a customer for what we make or for the service we provide. Sounds like common sense, doesn't it? And it is. But by the end of this chapter, many of you will be feeling it's not so simple.

I went for a cup of coffee and a wander around at this point. If you have been reading for a while, take a break also. You'll need to be fresh. While on the subject of wandering: I think one of the very best pieces of advice to managers is Tom Peters's MBWA: management by wandering around. It's good for you; it's good for your people. I rarely returned from one of my wanderings without having learned something; and I know that people at all levels of my various groups appreciated the personal contact.

———

It is vital to understand the customer concept if you and your group are going to be successful. The recovery efforts taking place in many large companies today are largely based on this seemingly simple concept, and many are requiring that their employees attend courses that all have the same generic theme as being presented here—satisfying the customer. If you are not currently in a backs-to-the-wall recovery mode, change course to this mode now, and perhaps avoid the trauma and cost of facing it later.

The customer concept seems simple. Most of us are in the business of providing either goods or services. If our customer is satisfied with those goods or services, then we are successful by one very important measure. Yet, in reality, it is very easy to lose track of what the customer really wants; and the longer it takes to realize it, the more customers one loses or alienates, and the longer it takes to recover. Fortunately, we are all in a position to experience daily what it takes to satisfy the customer because we are all customers ourselves at one time or another, and we know what gives us satisfaction: the car that finally gave us the reliability and quality we wanted, perhaps, the restaurant that consistently serves good food, the can opener that always works without slipping off, or the store salesclerk who was courteous and helpful.

These satisfactory experiences probably didn't come about by chance. If you were to look into the reason for your satisfaction, you would in almost all cases find it came about by design—because the people responsible for providing the item or service made a deliberate effort to find out what it would take to satisfy the customer.

And so it has to be with whatever you do if you want to be successful. I could list many examples of companies that ran into difficulties because they lost sight of the customer-satisfaction concept, but you know many of them already, and in most cases, they have been hammered from all corners and are doing something about it. And good luck to them; it takes a while to turn it around. Let's concentrate instead on doing it right in the first place, or catching it now before it's too late.

How about you who are currently managing something? Have you checked recently with your customer to see if you are providing what that customer wants? Have you *ever* asked your customer what he or she wanted? Or are you going along based on what you or your predecessors have judged to be what your customer needs? Be honest now. Unless you have spent some considerable time with your customers finding out what they need, then you can't say with certainty that you know. Therefore, there is a strong possibility you are not satisfying the customer. And lest I sound holier-than-thou in this area, let me assure you that I have drifted into this undesirable condition more than once. It is all too easy to conclude consciously or subconsciously that you can judge what the customer needs.

Now I'm going to complicate things by pointing out that most of you working in a manufacturing or service organization have two kinds of customers: (a) the *immediate customer(s)*, or the person or group next in line for your output and (b) the *ultimate customer*, or the consumer, the buyer, or lessor of the product or service the organization delivers. Most of us clearly understand the ultimate customer and the vital need to satisfy that customer's needs. Less well understood are the needs of the immediate customers, who are often other employees of the organization.

For example, the camera designer may know from the marketing group (immediate customer) what features are needed by photographers (ultimate customers). But has that designer spent enough time with the manufacturing people (immediate customer) to find out what *they* need? Perhaps they have plant limitations, shortages of certain skills, useable material left over from the last new product, or specific documentation requirements. The customer concept gets at this sometimes-neglected area of the immediate customer by making it part of normal procedure to (a) identify who *all* the customers are and (b) find out what they need and negotiate what can be done to meet their needs. Generally, the person or group to whom you directly provide goods or services and with whom you will negotiate relative to those goods and services is the immediate customer, or as stated above, the very next person or organization in line for your output.

Here are some further examples that may help illustrate the concept.

Supplier of Goods or Services	Immediate Customer	Ultimate Customer
Maker of Kenmore appliances	Sears Roebuck	You and me
Automobile design team	Automobile manu-facturing organization, marketing organization, etc.	You, me, Hertz, Avis, etc.
Operating-room nursing staff	Surgeons, hospital administration	Patient
Author	Publisher	Reader

Notice that in some cases, there is more than one immediate customer; that's quite common, and it doesn't make it any easier! But we can be very clear about one thing: *everyone* in the first two columns is responsible to the ultimate customer and must understand what those customers need. Often, the people in the first column need to meet directly with the people in the third column to satisfy that end. But the immediate customer is the one directly in line for your goods or services and the one with whom you will be working to ensure that your output is satisfactory. The engineer does not deal directly with the car buyer; the nursing staff does not negotiate operating-room support and services directly with the patients. Or in my case, although I want to give you the best little management book you can buy, I can't practically negotiate this with each of you individually: I do this by satisfying my immediate customer, my publisher.

I have learned that groups may have a very difficult time agreeing on the customer definition. This seems particularly so where companies have used the terms *primary* and *secondary* customers, and where the ultimate customer sometimes ends up classified as secondary—something that many find philosophically unsatisfactory. Hopefully, my definitions of *immediate* and *ultimate* customer may make this task much easier. Whichever terms you use, don't worry if your initial definitions seem to miss the mark; the right ones will become apparent to you when you start to think about who you will negotiate with for your services (next chapter). Meantime, you have made more progress than you might immediately think just by raising consciousness about customers and what they mean to you!

What should you do with this new-found knowledge? Just pause to think about it. This chapter had a few simple purposes: to introduce the concept of the two kinds of customers, to raise your consciousness about the need to ensure that both are satisfied, and to tell you that the chances of satisfying the ultimate customer are considerably enhanced by satisfying the immediate customer—with the added bonus of a more efficient, more economical, better-coordinated work force. In the following chapter, we'll take the concept through the next steps.

6

Customer Needs

I will assume that the last chapter has helped you understand who your customers are. That was step one of a four-step process. In this chapter, we'll look at the next three steps. They are all common sense in nature. Again, many companies who are currently going through a corrective or recovery phase have thoroughly formalized steps very similar to these.

Do you really need to do this? I would say that unless you are a one-person organization with direct line to your customer—for example, a hot dog vendor on the corner of Fifth and Main—the chances are that the process will expose some things you had never thought about or things you thought about but never pursued systematically.

If you are starting from scratch, you will benefit greatly by going through these steps. If you have been underway for some time, you also will probably benefit. The steps are summarized as follows:

1 Identify the customer (covered in the previous chapter).

2 Identify the customer needs.

3 Identify what your group can provide *to* the customer and what it needs *from* the customer.

4 Negotiate any gap between what the customer needs and what your group can provide; get agreement on your needs from the customer.

Seems reasonable, doesn't it. But just like identification of the customer, discussed in the last chapter, the responses are often assumed and sooner or later, you run into trouble.

You might go about addressing these points in several ways. You can do it quietly by yourself and dump the results on your group; you can prepare by yourself and then go through it from the beginning with the group; or you can just go to the group with a blank mind, a sheet of paper, and start.

I personally lean toward the second approach—preparing myself by thinking through the probable right responses, but then meeting with the group to develop the responses jointly starting at step number one. But that's because I don't consider myself particularly fast on my feet, and preparing in this way helps me keep the meeting on course and productive (as long as I take care to avoid being biased by my own preparation and remain open to accepting the group input). You may be very accomplished at thinking on your feet while hitting a new topic with a large group; if so, go for it. Both approaches beat the first one mentioned (doing it yourself and dumping it on the group) in terms of the commitment and trust you will obtain from the group.

Everyone in the group must attend the meeting. If the group is large, however, break it into teams with one spokesperson each. Have each team work through the questions, and have the spokesperson present the team's output. Do use a flip chart or some similar means to display the main points and the output of the group. Don't expect to get through it all at one sitting; in fact, to get the full range of responses by members of the group and yourself may require some expeditions to talk to the customer.

I can't prescribe exactly how these meetings should run; the potential variety of circumstances, tasks, and types of groups are obviously infinite (but do check out a later chapter on meetings and how to run them). I can say with confidence that if you go after these four key points in whatever way makes sense for you and yours, you will have an excellent base on which to build a successful group performance. In fact, this stage of development is so important that if you don't feel confident doing it on your own, you might want to consider getting outside help.

Let's take a look at how this meeting might go:

The agenda should follow the form of the four steps. You will have to judge how long each step will take. If the group's task is relatively uncomplicated, about an hour each should do it. If more complicated, each step may take as much as a half day—in which case we are obviously looking at four meetings. Never go more than four hours at one time; even then, allow at least one break. My own preference for meetings is that they run generally no longer than two hours (which comes of admitting to my own attention-span limitations). However, the returns anticipated from this particular meeting may justify a somewhat longer engagement.

First you will want to explore the question of who is the customer (as we did in the last chapter). And, based on what you learned from the last chapter, you will have to coach your people into understanding the concept. Anticipate some serious questions about the definition of immediate and ultimate customers. Make sure you understand the difference by studying the last chapter again, and do your best to enlighten the group. But, if the group strongly objects to your definition, don't dig in regardless. If their concept seems slightly wrong to you, it will probably wash out later; meanwhile, you've had a very useful and enlightening discussion that has aroused people's thinking and sensitized them to a vitally important issue.

Now you can tackle what the customer wants. I'm going to assume that your group has a reasonable grasp of what the ultimate customer's needs are and, from here on, I'm referring to the immediate customer. (If, of course, you happen to be the lead marketing organization of a company, you will be more directly concerned with the ultimate customer.)

Make a commitment at this point to address the needs of the immediate customer. In fact, for more complex organizations, you may want to pause after the first meeting and have some or all of the group go out to the customer first— to find out firsthand what the customer wants. *Whichever way you do it, do not rely solely on your perception or the group's perception of what the customer wants.*

In step three, you and your group will need to review the customer's needs to see if you can match them with what you can deliver; there may be gaps. Identify the gaps, and start a process to see what you can do to close them; treat it like problem solving (see chapter 10), but don't expect to solve them all on this first meeting. Also, identify what you need from the customer (for example, your customer may want something done faster; you, in response, may need to request clearer or more timely indications of needs).

Step four involves negotiation with the customer; and since a group effort isn't practical here, this task falls mainly on your shoulders—perhaps accompanied by a small support group. You have worked the gaps as best you can, and you have identified the group's needs. You now have to talk all this through with the customer and develop a good working agreement and set of mutual expectations. How well this goes will depend on your skills as a communicator and, perhaps, as a negotiator. You have two things going for you: (1) you have done your homework as described, so you know what you are talking about and (2) you almost cannot help but achieve a marked improvement in mutual understanding with your customer.

Next? Communicate the outcome with your people, put into operation whatever you have jointly developed, work out the remaining issues (there are always some), and do it again whenever you sense the need, whenever you get a hint that a gap has opened between customer needs and what you are delivering, and whenever the group turnover or expansion has reached a point where some significant part of the group has not been exposed to this process.

The following simulated case history is intended to illustrate the teachings of this and the previous chapter. For clarity I have chosen a relatively small organization, and the negotiations you will read about are admittedly concluded in relative ease.

SITUATION

Sally is the manager of the dining room in the Majestic Hotel. Jack is the chef. Both have recently been to a course given by Majestic Hotels of America, Inc., where among other things, they learned about the customer concept. Sally has concerns about the breakfast service, and she and Jack are meeting to discuss them. In this organization,

˙ Sally and Jack each report directly to the hotel manager. Their conversation is divided into the four steps discussed at the beginning of the chapter:

1. Identify the Customer

Sally: Hi, Jack. How did you enjoy the course?

Jack: Well, it opened my eyes. You know, I never thought of you as my customer—my immediate customer that is. But it makes sense; you are closer to the ultimate customers and probably have the best day-to-day awareness of what they need and what pleases them.

Sally: I guess I, too, was surprised at the relationship they were proposing until I saw the sense of it. But we both have the same ultimate customer—our guests and others who eat here. And that is what I wanted to talk to you about.

Jack: OK, what's up?

2. Identify the Customer Needs

Sally: Well, the hotel manager recently gave me a copy of a survey indicating that we are not meeting all our customers' needs at breakfast time. Many of them, particularly family groups, don't like paying seven to ten dollars for breakfast—when beverage, taxes, and tip are included—and they go elsewhere for something cheaper. Then we have business people who are usually on a tight schedule and don't want to sit around waiting to be served—especially when they are by themselves. I had one rather irate businesswoman tell me she was going to stay at a Roosters' Hotel next time, because there she can just serve herself with coffee, juice, cereals, or pastry and be on her way.

Jack: But we put in the buffet for that kind of customer.

Sally: Well, we thought it was for that kind of customer, I agree. But the survey indicates otherwise; it indicates that people's views about health are changing, and many don't like the idea of paying seven dollars to load up their plate with more food than they want to eat.

Jack: Well, we've always prided ourselves on providing an elegant breakfast dining experience, but I have noticed when I look out into the dining room at breakfast, it's rarely more than half full; maybe the survey is telling us why. Well, OK, what do you think you need?

Sally: I think I need a couple of things. First of all, I need something to accommodate those who just want to grab coffee, juice, and a pastry—and want to consume it in a comfortable little area or just run with it. I don't think we can make it free, but maybe we could make a nominal charge—something less than two dollars. I think we can convert one side of the buffet for this, but I'll need you to supply the food and beverages for it. Also, I think I need to add some simpler, lower-cost items to the menu—some that I can list in the three-to-five-dollar range. You could help me with some suggestions there. Then we need to speed up the service generally. I had breakfast at a restaurant recently, and I really appreciated the fact that as I was being seated, I was immediately offered coffee or tea to drink while I was studying the menu. Since the waiters work for me, I can do something about that. But I would like your thoughts on what might be done to speed up delivery of the food after the waiter has placed the order.

Jack: Wow, that's a lot to think about.

Sally: I know. Look, take the survey, read it yourself, and let's get together again on Tuesday to see what you can come up with. Oh, by the way, whatever we come up with shouldn't cost more. We have a profit squeeze also; it's in the survey report.

3. Identify What the Group Can Do

Jack: Hi, Sally. Tuesday came around awfully quickly, but I think I've got something for you.

Sally: OK, I'm anxious to hear it.

Jack: Well, I got together with the kitchen staff and kicked it around a bit. You know, it's a funny thing, but none of them were very surprised about it. One of them even came up with a name for the beverage and pastry line: the Fast Lane. Anyway, we thought of a good selection of lower-cost menu items that I think will fit into your lower price range—even some specially for kids. However, we will not be able to speed up service from the kitchen if we bake our own pastries, so we suggest that we buy them from a local bakery; if the report is right, the increased sales should more than off-set that cost. Also, we'd have no problem stocking any extra beverage supplies.

Sally: Sounds good so far. What do you think you might be able to contribute to faster service?

4. Negotiation

Jack: That wasn't so easy—especially with the additional work needed to provide additional lower-cost menu items and to stock the Fast Lane. And because profits are a concern, I didn't want to think about adding more people at this time. But the staff pointed out that they spend a lot of time making more coffee and taking it out to the buffet, pouring cereal into bowls, and so on. So the question is, could your waiters also take on a little more and be responsible for maintaining the coffee supplies and serving the cereals?

Sally: I think they can; I'll look into it with them. But I need one more thing from you.

Jack: Go ahead.

Sally: Well, we are going to have to take all this up to the hotel manager for approval. Would you get me actual numbers on buying the pastries? I want to be very sure of the numbers when we put forth our proposal.

Jack: OK. Will do. And after that meeting, I suggest we also meet with all our people to let them know the outcome. Oh, and just one more thing.

Sally: Yes, Jack?

Jack: Would you have any objection if I wandered out into the dining room now and again to talk to the customers?

Sally: Absolutely not, Jack. I'll be wandering around more myself in the future.

———

I chose the above simulation because I wanted something familiar to most of you—so that you could concentrate on the process and not on the subject matter. I'm sure some hotel employees would be very willing to show me how much more complicated it could get!

Beyond illustrating the process, I hope some other things came across in this simulated discussion. Consider the following questions:

1 Do you think the discussion went better because both Sally and Jack went to the training course?

2 Did Sally take any unfair advantage of her new-found role as customer?

3 Did she just tell Jack what to do, or did she tell him what she felt she needed after reading the survey and then ask him to participate in addressing the issues?

4 Did Jack just go off into a corner and come up with proposals, or did he engage the experience of the people who work for him?

5 Were Jack's people surprised at the results of the survey?

I'm sure most readers saw these as rhetorical questions, and I ask them merely to emphasize the positive behavior demonstrated in this little simulation. However, the last question (5) does require further comment. (In the simulation, Jack discovered that his people were not surprised at the survey content.) I have known many situations in which the manager is the last to recognize a problem—perhaps due to preoccupation with administrative matters, perhaps due to complacency, perhaps due to a hope-it-goes-away posture. Whatever the reason, I must stress here, as elsewhere in this book, the need to recognize and focus the talents that exist in your group and to stay in touch with the feelings of the individuals in the group. I once witnessed a big organizational-efficiency and morale-improvement effort conducted by a very high-level manager. His diagnosis of the problems was unusually fast and accurate—mainly due to his willingness to engage with people at *all* levels of the organization.

Some readers might insist that the two characters in the restaurant illustration would, surely, have had this kind of interaction *without* having experienced the training. My response is *maybe*. Note the information at the beginning of the story that the two people involved each reported directly to the hotel manager. Sally was not Jack's manager, and the organizational structure did not make it a requirement that these two people have this conversation; the fact is that the bigger the organization, the less likely it is that this kind of exchange takes place.

Let's look at another example. This time, I will not simulate the situation but draw from my experience with two companies who design and build office equipment.

The field service organization of Company A, after many years of frustration, made it known to the design department that the technicians were fed up with carrying around so many tools. One of the more straightforward of the reasons for their frustration was that each designer responsible for a part of the machine had his or her own favorite choice of fasteners. For example, some might specify hexagon-headed bolts requiring a wrench; some might specify slotted screws or Phillips-head screws that required two kinds of screwdrivers; some would specify hexagon socket screws (for those unfamiliar with hexagon socket screws, they have a cylindrical head with a deep hexagonal-shaped cavity; to loosen or tighten them requires a bunch of tools made from a hexagonal rod: each one only fits one screw size).

Perhaps without realizing it, the field service people were pioneering the immediate and ultimate customer concept. Following is a simplified account of what took place next:

1   Field service workers made it clear how much the design affected the time it took them to service the machines (thus identifying themselves as an immediate customer).

2 Field service asked for *one* type and size of screw throughout the machine (thus stating a customer need).

3 Design department members reviewed field service's needs, found they couldn't reduce to *one* type and size of fastener due to varying strength and duty requirements for fasteners in the machine, but came back with a proposal to drastically reduce the number of sizes (thus identifying what the group can do).

4 Both parties got together and further agreed to phase out one type of screw altogether (thus negotiating the gaps).

The result was an increase in immediate customer satisfaction, accompanied by decreased costs to the company due to the reduction in service time. The ultimate customer also benefited due to reduction in time the machine was out of operation.

Today, Company A routinely goes through its own version of the customer-concept process, and this kind of situation is much less likely to develop. Looking at the example in hindsight, one can easily observe that, surely, what Company A did was just common sense. My response is that, particularly in a large organization, this kind of common-sense interaction may not take place unless some process is in place to encourage it. For instance, during the time I was writing this book, I was involved peripherally with Company B, which was in the last design phase for a new machine—just before going to production. I discovered that it had not yet engaged its field service organization (immediate customers), and thus, did not fully understand their needs. Without some rapid corrective action, the service provisions would have clearly fallen short; it would have been just a question of how much.

In summary, work with your group. Develop a good understanding of who your immediate and ultimate customers are, what their needs are, and how you can best meet these needs. In so doing, you bring *all* the group's talent to bear on this vital aspect and will develop not only a sound base for the group's future success but also a sense of involvement and commitment.

You may initially think that this process doesn't fit your particular operation, and in some cases, it may not. But be aware that many large companies that did not see the need for a process like this in the past are now using it as a significant part of a turnaround activity. Even if you end up making no changes in what you are doing or intending to do, the discussions that the process stimulates will enlighten everyone involved. (For instance, I can almost guarantee you a variety of perceptions within your group on customers' needs!) Negotiating the group output with your customer will probably not be a shoe-in, but it will undoubtedly result in improved mutual understanding, which in itself, is an achievement that will surely pave the way for increased satisfaction on both sides. Whenever possible, have your people visit with the customers and talk directly to them. This encounter provides valuable insights and greatly enhances awareness of issues that even the most conscientious immediate customer may not bring to the table.

Here's a good place to take another break, because we are going to shift direction in the next chapter. There, we'll focus on key skills that a successful manager must possess and continuously upgrade in order to meet the daily demands of the leadership role.

7

Decision Making

Decisions come in all types and sizes. But have you noticed that the process of decision making often lacks the thoroughness commensurate with the potential consequences of the decision? For example, a person who agrees to buy several thousand dollars worth of stock after a brief talk with a stockbroker might then spend several weeks doing exhaustive research before buying a five-hundred-dollar stereo. But how does one systematically go about making decisions? Well, from one who admits to not always doing it systematically or consistently (although I was pleased with the stereo!), let me try and draw from experience of good and bad decision making to help you find the right way for you. From time to time, lacking consensus on some aspect, your group is going to look to their leader for a decision. Your inability to make one probably will lose you more respect than making a bad one.

First of all, let me say that if you are spending most of the day making decisions for people, you are not managing effectively. Specifically, you are not effectively using the talents of the people who work for you. Your mode of operation should be this: let your people make most of the decisions affecting daily operations while you reserve a select few that you judge to be sufficiently grave or strategically important enough to the group or the parent enterprise to need your personal involvement.

So often I have been in a manager's office when one of his or her people comes in and says something like this: "The widget on number two fell off, and number three is overdue for maintenance. Which one should we use?" And the manager bites on it, like a hungry fish bites on bait, and delivers a decision. And many times, this is just the wrong thing to do. Unless this person is so lacking in intelligence or ability to come up with the right decision, or at least come up with the facts and a recommendation, you should avoid the temptation to make one for them. Oh, let's be honest. It's sometimes a very satisfying thing to do—good for the ego, sort of macho, the feeling of being needed, and all that stuff. But you are running the risk of retarding a person's growth and making your own life a hotbed of seat-of-the-pants decision making; for if this is your way of operating, you may not have the time to make well-considered decisions in every case.

What to do? People who worked for me soon understood that they did not come to me for a decision unless they had thought it through themselves and had some recommendations on what the decision should be. After all, it was in their best interests that I didn't go off half-cocked on a matter that concerned them so closely! And after all, I would think, am I so all-powerful and wise that I can routinely make decisions for people who are invariably much closer to the facts than I am? The manager's job is to see that good decisions get made; that involves showing people how to make them when appropriate and how to prepare for a decision when it does appear appropriate for the manager to have the final word.

Notice I said *good decisions* and not *right decisions*. I will always remember being at a meeting where it was painfully obvious we were in trouble because one of the people in the room had made the *wrong decision* some time back. The senior manager in the room said to that person, "I don't expect you to always make the right decision. I do expect you to make the best decision you can based on the facts you have before you at the time. In my opinion, and given the facts you had at your disposal, you made that best decision." Think about that. Most of us fear making the wrong decision, and even if we can't use this little story to rationalize our own situation, we *must* keep it in mind when judging the decision making of others—that is, we must keep hindsight in its place. The decision for Ford to build the Edsel, for Xerox to get into computers, for you to trade in your trusty old car for a new lemon can probably be considered wrong decisions; *but* they all may have been the *best* decision when the decision was made, and that is as much as anyone should expect of you.

So, you and/or yours have to make a decision. What to do? Well, it's simple; you look at the alternatives, weigh their pros and cons, and chose the best-looking one. Now that's what you call being trite! And yet that's what it usually comes down to; whether it's a decision to buy a new radio or repair the old one or a decision by one company to buy another. The major difference is in the amount of information gathering and the time taken to reach a decision.

In the next few pages, I'll present one way to assemble the important facts involved in a decision and to review these facts in a way that will *help* you make a decision. I have used it often and regretted *not* using it just about as often. It can be fitted to most situations. There is a simple mathematical computation as part of the process, *but do not get carried away by the mathematical solution.* If it doesn't feel right, go back and review the content of your analysis. This is where, I think, *Consumer Reports* does such an outstanding job: it shows us what selection factors or attributes we should think about before deciding on something. If we don't agree with their conclusion, it doesn't mean that either of us is wrong; it probably means we put different weightings on one or more of the attributes.

Following is the approach I like to use when I need to assemble a number of factors (in this case, attributes) in a fashion that will help me make a good decision. The method is loosely based on something taught by Kepner-Tregoe Associates. I learned it quite early in my career, and it has stood the test of time very well indeed. In this case, I used it to make a choice (and, therefore, a decision) on a new car purchase. I had already made a gross cut (the Lamborghini and the Yugo were the first to go) and had got it down to a short list of two; but there is no limit to the number of choices you can handle with this approach.

Now, on to the chart, the key to this whole process, and then I'll explain what it all means.

Attribute	Weight	Car A	Car B	Comments
Reliability	9	10 (90)	10 (90)	Both above average in *Consumer Reports* and other sources
Handling	10	9 (90)	9 (90)	Based on test drive
Engine	10	7 (70)	10 (100)	B has turbo—wow! A doesn't offer it.
Stereo	7	2 (14)	7 (49)	A has two speakers in doors; B has speakers in dash.
Fuel economy	8	9 (72)	8 (64)	
Price	7	9 (63)	8 (56)	
Totals		**399**	**449**	

All right, let's see what happened here.

First, I set down the attributes that were important to me. Then I weighted them in terms of how important they were to me (most important = 10, least = 1). As you can see, I am hungry for power and performance, and as I am screaming around the back roads I like to listen to a decent sound system. I also would prefer an exciting car that has a very occasional malfunction to one that is dull but never goes wrong. Cost is important, but not overwhelmingly so in this case since I had already ruled out the Lamborghini. Weightings are necessary when the attributes are not of equal importance (and they're usually not).

Next, I scored each car (Car A and Car B) against each attribute; the better it met the requirements, the higher the score. (I suggest a range of 1–10 for scores and weighting; it's easy to think in these terms, and you have reasonably convenient numbers to mess with later when you have to do a little math.)

As you can see, both scored a 10 on reliability; both were well above average in *Consumer Reports* and other sources of information. (Ignore the two entries of 90 for the time being.) In the area of engine performance, it was very clear; the engine in Car A was a bit above average while the engine in Car B lived up to my dreams. Thus, Car A scored 7 while Car B scored 10. (Again ignore the numbers 70 and 100 for the time being.)

As for the stereo, I played around for a long time with my existing car, trying to get a pleasing sound distribution (the two front speakers were in the front doors), and concluded it couldn't be done without extensive changes. Since Car B already had the speakers high on the dash where I wanted them, it was a "no-contest."

Having completed the scoring, I then multiplied each score by the weighting for that attribute to arrive at the weighted score; shown in parentheses. This step resulted in weighted scores that related to the degree of importance I had placed on each individual attribute. Then I added all these weighted scores to arrive at the numerical result, which as you can see, came out in favor of Car B.

Then, and this is most important, I sat back and thought about whether the answer made good sense. Did it confirm my gut intuition? If it didn't, I should go back and reexamine the attributes. Maybe they are not all there, or maybe I should reexamine the scoring or weighting. *Never accept the mathematical answer if you don't feel comfortable with it.* If, for example, this was a decision between two kidney dialysis machines then clearly, a weighting of 10 would be appropriate for reliability; in fact, you would probably not even proceed with the rest of the analysis if this particular attribute did not score a perfect 10. Or if someone was buying a car under very limited budget conditions, then the price would receive higher weighting. Let your gut have its say.

This is only one decision-making tool; but it is simple, expedient, and applicable to a wide variety of decisions. By all means, go to some decision-making courses, especially if a decision involves a great deal of money. But even when you have learned all about NPVs (net present value) and ROIs (return on investment), you'll still have to make a choice, and a method like that shown is still valid—perhaps even more so since the financials are usually only one attribute to consider. Indeed, guard against being overwhelmed by the results of a financial analysis. Presumably it was a financial analysis that convinced a certain faucet manufacturer to change the spherical portion of its valve mechanism from steel to plastic; and it was probably consumer dissatisfaction with this plastic part's disintegration that led the manufacturer to return to steel.

Just to help you get started, here are a few examples and some corresponding attributes you might consider in making a decision:

— Buying a new home versus enlarging: cost, degree to which needs will be met, future value, school district, property taxes, maintenance costs for the next ten years, financing terms, neighborhood

— Promoting person A, B, or C: qualifications for the job, previous work record, ability to get along with and motivate people, knowledge of the job, attitude about the organization, whether they have read this book

— Choosing between several pieces of equipment: degree to which they satisfy requirements (better find out and be clear what the requirements are), cost (nearly always in the list), reliability, ease of use, compatibility with existing equipment

— Choosing between project approach A and B: degree to which objectives potentially met, technical risk, cost of project over life, schedule and time to market, build costs, service or warranty costs, potential profit (avoid double counting relative to these last three), market share, company-reputation enhancement

Get the idea? As an alternative, you will occasionally come across a decision involving only a few attributes, in which case you can use a simple matrix to get organized. Here's one example:

	What's good about it?	What's bad about it?
Promote Mary		
Promote John		

Fill in the matrix as best you can, lean back, and ponder. Ponder which is the right choice, or whether you perhaps need the extra detail of the previous approach, or whether you need to sleep on it—often a good interim action.

In my very first management course (Management Discussion Skills—if it's still around, get it!), I learned two questions, to be asked in succession, that can be very revealing when choosing between actions: (1) How does this help? and (2) How does this not help? They are so simple, but you may be surprised what you get out of these two questions. And they're good for group sessions, too.

I also like the two columns a friend of mine set up to help him decide whether to quit a company he was working for. He headed one column *reasons for staying,* the other, *reasons for leaving.* He came up with one reason for staying and twenty-eight for leaving. That certainly sharpened up his thinking, and the decision, of course, wasn't difficult.

In summary, you need to make it clear that you are willing to let your people make decisions but that you are capable and willing to make decisions yourself when it is clearly your final responsibility. Don't fall into the trap of letting people dump their decision-making requirements on you; you stifle their growth and risk your own. Decisions, by definition, involve making choices. Arraying the choices in a structured manner can help you make that decision. Choosing the attributes, or important factors, is half the battle, since that activity in itself helps to bring things into perspective and render the decision manageable. The method suggested is a valid one whether you are choosing between four radios to buy (the chart can have any number of columns) or between merging your billion dollar company with another; the main difference is in the amount of information gathering.

8

Meetings

Just mentioning the word *meeting* can set off a flood of emotions—many of them negative. Typically, people respond with the following negative descriptions: waste of time, boring, stressful, threatening, more bloody paperwork, takes me a week to pull my stuff together, it beats working, why are we meeting? and so on.

What to do? Well, first of all, consider whether some or all of the above reactions are valid and justified in the organization you manage. I feel quite safe in assuming that at least one of them is, and in many cases, several of them. I also feel very strongly that meetings are essential. Among the reasons: they provide opportunities for clear and timely communications on matters important to the group and for some parts of a decision-making process.

Let's take a look at the objections raised in the first paragraph. First, they surely can be a waste of time—and, therefore, money. Consider a four-hour meeting for twenty people whose average salary is $30,000 per year (which means the true cost per year to the organization is probably more than $40,000 per year when all benefits and overheads are accounted for). This meeting is running about $400 per hour, or a total cost of about $1600—expensive if not much is being accomplished! This doesn't necessarily suggest it's a bad deal. It could, in fact, be an excellent return on investment. And that's what it's all about really —making sure that the meeting is necessary, that the necessary people are there, and that the meeting process is efficient.

Generally, a meeting should be preceded by a communication that defines a specified purpose, an agenda, and time allocations for the items on the agenda. This should be done if only as a courtesy and a gesture of respect for the attendees. Specifically, it attunes people in advance, enables preparation to help ensure the necessary facts are on hand, and enables participants to gauge their own contribution to fit the allotted time. A useful adjunct that is taught in many operational-improvement courses is to ask for additional agenda items at the beginning of the meeting; again, the submitter must state the purpose and time required, and the meeting leader may have to judge whether the meeting can expand sufficiently to absorb the extra items or whether to carry them over to another time.

Now, I did start the preceding paragraph with *generally.* Occasionally it's OK to set a meeting without requiring the preparations. Sometimes you may need to kick something off with a *group grope,* for example, where the topic is so new that the purpose of the meeting is merely to start to grapple with something in the hopes that a direction will emerge. Probably, the overall purpose of the meeting will be clear, but the meeting itself will be mainly concerned with clarifying the objectives, finding out what is known and what is not known, and then defining an agenda for another meeting. Such meetings are inevitable and necessary; in these situations, it is foolish to try for any real structure—after all, freewheeling has its place. However, the intent should be to expediently move into a mode with structure. Future meetings should begin to show specific directions, or the sessions will quickly lose a sense of purpose.

Another class of meeting I would like to cover is the routine-communications meeting. It is virtually impossible to ensure adequate, timely, and equitable levels of communication to all group members without such meetings. Memos can occasionally suffice, but they lack important features such as two-way communication, group interactions, and information sharing. I was once discouraged by grumbling about my own regularly held full-group meetings, and I let the meetings fade away. Then one day, one of my people said to me, "You know, I really miss the group meeting. I don't feel as if I know enough about all that's going on." Shortly thereafter, I reinstated the meetings.

I recommend that you commit yourself to holding these routine-communications meetings and apply some of the same rules you would apply to other meetings. For example, you should have an agenda with times allotted. But by all means, be imaginative with the content. Make sure some of your people have a spot on the agenda to talk about an activity or experience that is of interest to others in the group. And the topics don't all have to be absolutely project related. I see nothing wrong with spending 10 percent of the meeting time on a topic of more general and personal interest. I myself gained some slight notoriety for my pitch on the economic benefits of the 401K savings scheme; and although I did get one or two leg pulls about it, my secretary advised me a day or two later that the supply of application forms had suddenly been cleaned out.

The bean counters are going to question how I rationalize using 10 percent of the meeting in this way, given my previous scoping of the hourly cost of meetings. And I'm going to wave my arms around a bit and talk about *intangibles*—things that you can't put numbers on. For if, by this means, I raised the level of interest in the meeting and increased the sense of sharing within the group, then I say that was a good deal!

Now back to basics. Always prepare for your meetings. If you need a projector make sure well before the meeting that it will be available, and make sure it works and that a spare bulb is available. Even check to be sure the room has been vacated—or will be by the time you need it. Do these things to avoid getting off to a scrappy start from which it's sometimes difficult to recover. Particularly when the meeting is critical, I visit the room once or twice prior to the meeting to ensure its readiness. For the people on the receiving end, the occasional lapses due to lack of preparation tend to be a giggle at first, but eventually they become just plain tiresome and leave a negative impression of the meeting leader's organizational capabilities.

And start on time. Waiting for latecomers hurts in two ways: it actually rewards the latecomers while punishing the punctual. Also, make it known that you consider the success of the meeting to be everyone's responsibility. Encourage people to speak up when it appears the meeting is getting off track or otherwise giving a poor return for the time being expended.

As noted in the complaints list at the beginning of this chapter, people don't only characterize meetings as a waste of time, but as stressful and threatening. Certainly meetings can be stressful; if things aren't going well in a group, stress can't be avoided. In better times, though, stress can be of the self-induced kind (that is, conscientious people will generate their own stress level). However, as the manager, you should work to prevent the meeting from becoming a threatening arena. This is something you must control by your own actions and those of other meeting members. It is unacceptable, for example, to bawl someone out in a meeting. I'll repeat: *unacceptable!* If you have serious questions to raise, by all means do this at the meeting, where it is important for all to share the knowledge; but if you feel the need to question someone's competency or to heavily criticize, then do it in privacy after the meeting. To do it in the meeting is unnecessarily demoralizing both for the target of your anger and for the rest of the group; your people will mentally put on a suit of armor, and in the long run, you lose. Similarly, you must check border skirmishes that bubble up between group members.

It is also important to pull in the contributions of meeting attendees. We all vary in our degree of spontaneous verbal contribution. I, for example, admit to having my bad days, when I tend to withdraw at meetings or don't feel the need to add my thoughts. But they may well be needed, and I may be letting the group down by being so reticent. If I am unduly withdrawn, and the meeting leader feels I might have something to contribute, he or she should directly ask me for my views on the topic. The point here is that it is very important to be on the lookout for those who may have something to contribute but may be holding back.

See to it that nobody leaves one of your meetings without offering something to the group. The corollary to this—in a meeting on a specific topic—is that if a person really does have nothing to offer, your invitee list needs fixing:

one deadly sin is to waste the time of people at meetings where they cannot contribute. (This doesn't apply to routine-communications meetings, of course.)

For a, perhaps, rather bizarre example of turning a negative meeting into a positive one, let me tell you about a real-life story which involved me when I was working for a relatively large company. During the early days of manufacture of a new product, this company commonly held *sunrise meetings,* or sessions in which the manufacturing engineering, design engineering, and service engineering folks got together daily to discuss the previous day's production difficulties and resolve them. The term *sunrise* relates to the fact that these meetings were usually scheduled for 7:00 A.M. One meeting I attended felt like a battleground; instead of engaging in a joint problem-solving session, people spent much of the meeting trading shots as they attempted to blame the problems on the other camp. As a consequence, most people became very defensive, and some became very creative in finding excuses for not attending the meeting.

One morning, having mentally gone through my "flight or fight" decision-making exercise, I decided to do neither, but instead, observed the game being played out. I then thought that since it was indeed some kind of game, it should have rules with a consistent scoring method. So, later that day, I developed the rules you will find on the next page. Basically, I awarded points whenever one side fired a shot. The number of points to be awarded depended on matching the shot to a descriptor in the rules. Go ahead, look at the rules now.

———

DESIGN
ENGINEERING

MANUFACTURING
ENGINEERING

Field service engineering
sheltering from fallout

THE SHOT-TRADING GAME: RULES

Type of Shot	Description	Points
Blue shot	A "shot from the blue." One side brings in problem they attribute to other side. The other side is totally surprised and unable to respond or defend.	10
Blue shot with counter	Similar to above, but other side instinctively counter-attacks strongly and manages to throw doubt on side responsible for the problem.	5
Grudge shot	Member of one side slams other side with insult based on nothing specific but on a long-term mistrust of other side's organization.	4
Cheap shot	Member of one side is having a bad day; got up early and missed breakfast. Attacks member of other side with random accusation.	2
Cheap shot w/ counter	Similar to above, but connects with member of other side whose demeanor is about the same and shows it with approximately equivalent accusation.	1
No shot	One member from each side jointly describes problem and how they got together to solve it.	0

With the program chief's consent, I presented the rules and scoring method at the next morning's meeting. People were sceptical at first, but the effect of the rules on this first meeting was magical. Consciousness of shots was raised dramatically, and several times people asked me to judge the appropriate number of points to be awarded. Or someone might say, "Sounds like a five-pointer to me," much to everyone's amusement. At the end of the meeting, the tension was noticeably less. Someone asked me for the final score, and I replied that I had not really found a need to keep score. Nobody complained. The meetings continued on an uptrend; an occasional lapse would bring forth a reminder of the rules from somebody, and we would resume a constructive dialogue.

Not quite the end of the story. I ran into the program chief about two years later. He had reached the same stage on another program. At one point in our discussion he said, "By the way... uhm... do you still have a copy of that silly game?"

The game achieved many things. For one thing, it conveyed the significance of the behavior related to the scores of ten and zero. But perhaps the most important thing it did—through the expedient of poking fun at ourselves—was to raise our sensitivity to the difference between constructive and destructive behavior toward each other and to unite us as a team with common objectives.

This is not intended to suggest a universal approach to improving meetings that have strayed off course; it is offered as a real-life example that may stimulate your thinking concerning your own meetings and what you may need to do about them. Whether you use this approach or something similar, it will require careful judgment about the circumstances, the people involved, and your ability to carry it off; like most things where gains are being sought, there is some risk attached also. If you should attempt something similar, I do recommend that you make it clear you want to improve the *meeting*, not the people attending it. The focus has to be on improving this impersonal thing called a *meeting*, or you may stir up feelings of resentment—perhaps justifiably so if you have been the person responsible for calling this meeting for some time.

I should point out that seminars and other educational programs exist to educate *all* people of a group in the most productive meeting conduct. If you are heavily meeting oriented, *and if the meetings are truly necessary,* you might consider the additional gains offered by such programs.

In summary, first think carefully about the need for a meeting. If it concerns communications, but you are not sure it's necessary, do it anyway! It's rare that communication is overdone, and for many communications, a memo just doesn't do it. Next, be sure attendees know the purpose of the meeting, and be sure the right people are invited (that is, people who *must* hear the proceedings and people who *can* contribute). In addition, publish an agenda before the meeting, and add to it as necessary as a first order of business at the actual meeting. Allot times to agenda items, enlist the help of an attendee to call time, and be sure to *pull in* the reticent. Finally, summarize at the end. Above all, prepare, prepare, prepare.

Specific action is required if your meetings need improving. While I don't recommend universal application of "the game," you might consider having your whole group attend a good educational program on meeting organization and participation.

You might find the following checklist useful:

Preparation

— Reserve room or other suitable space.

— Order refreshments if appropriate.

— Circulate an agenda showing topics and allotted time.

— Order or have on hand audiovisual aids if required.

— Talk to people you have asked to present something to ensure you both understand what is required.

— Ensure you have thought through your part and have sufficient memory joggers on hand.

Last check

— See that the room is truly vacated.

— See that all things ordered or reserved as above have arrived.

Start-up

— Review agenda.

— Invite new agenda items, allocate time or list them for a future meeting.

— Appoint someone to call time per the agenda.

— Remind participants that *all present* are responsible for making this a good productive meeting.

During session

— Keep it focused; allow reasonable excursions, but don't allow them if they are leading nowhere and wasting valuable time.

— Encourage the meek-but-knowledgeable. Steer but don't crush the overexuberant.

— Stay on time (your timekeeper is of enormous help here).

— Summarize each item to ensure common understanding.

— Assign follow-up actions to yourself or others when appropriate. Don't leave unanswered issues just lying there.

— Occasionally finish by asking attendees what was good and what was bad about the meeting. List in two columns on a blackboard or other visual aid.

Later

— Look at the two columns from the end-of-meeting list and think about your next meeting.

9

Planning

For most of us, unless a job is absolutely routine, some level of planning is necessary. In the case of a substantially new project, the plan *is* the project; and even in the case of a more routine operation, there must surely be a need for planning if the operation is to maintain or improve its performance. If things aren't planned, and planned intelligently, they either don't happen, or they happen in an unexpected way at an unexpected time.

I once took part in an investigation within a major corporation to find out why some products didn't get to the market on time. Poor planning was one of the top three causes: both lack of planning and unrealistic planning. The consequences of poor planning are particularly disastrous in organizations developing products. By the time people realize a delay is occuring, the number of people on the project is typically at its highest. Thus, conditions are perfect for a devastating combination: loss of market revenue combined with a very high *burn rate*—the dollars needed to keep everyone going even though some people further down the line are inevitably being paid just to wait.

But what effect does poor planning have on people? It's equally disastrous and, perhaps, of longer-term concern. You may be able to fix the financial problem with a visit to the bank, but the effect on the morale of the team involved in—but not necessarily responsible for—the failure can be much more lasting; I know of no quick fixes. And this may be the most devastating effect of all because of its insidious and typically long-standing effect on the future.

In almost all cases it is *irresponsible* to be lacking a plan and, moreover, an intelligent plan. Even if your business is making pizza, you would look pretty foolish without pepperoni on Friday night because you didn't order it on Tuesday—which was or should have been the plan, even if unstated.

(For the next few paragraphs I will be leaning toward my own experience in engineering, but I believe you can learn from this experience no matter what your organization does.)

It is unfortunate that when budget restrictions hit larger companies and they need to reduce resources, planners are among the first to be let go—even though the skills of an experienced planner may well be the single most important determinant of success in meeting objectives on time. When these people are let go, the assumption is that the people they previously supported will magically inherit those same planning skills, and everything will go on as before.

Well not quite, because all those people who previously had the planning support will now be doing their own thing. All those people include the optimists, the pessimists, the unwilling, the unrealistic, the brilliant free spirits who are unaware of other people's limitations, the conscientious but naive, and so on. Get the idea? No coordinated, integrated, consistent planning will take place. And even one lousy plan in a group of ten good ones can derail a project; the space shuttle doesn't leave the pad if the vacuum-dried food doesn't get there on time.

Well, that's the manager's job you might say (to ensure good planning). But managers are usually part of a team, too, and in that team there are probably the optimists, the pessimists, the unwilling, the brilliant free spirits ....

Let me now give you a taste of what a professional planner can do for a project. Again, I'm drawing from my real-life experience with high-technology projects, but most of you should be able to extrapolate. Following is a very simple-looking plan that might have been done by a quite competent engineer. It's a simple example of a plan-display approach known as a GANTT chart:

design: 4 months	build: 3 months	test: 3 months

Now let me tear into it. And believe me, I'm doing it based on real-life experience. The weaknesses I will expose are common ones, and they continue to show up.

1   Design, 4 months

— Will you have a concept chosen by day 1 and a design plan available so you don't spin your wheels at the start?

— Are you dependent on some other event or person in order to start?

— How many parts is the product likely to have? This one's a doozy. If you don't know or can't estimate the number, then you can't estimate a time. This is one of the most prevalent errors. Example: I met with an engineer to review his plan. He had estimated (guessed) three months to design and get the drawings out. We counted the number of parts, and it came to about 75. Using a metric I developed myself of 20 work hours per part (believe me, it is proven for this type of application), I came up with 1500 hours. Now, the average number of working hours per month is about 170. Thus, he would have needed to do about nine months work in three months. We were able to replan by dividing the work appropriately, and we headed off a disaster.

2   Build, 3 months

— Does the model shop have a work-load vacuum just waiting to suck up your job the minute you drop the drawings on them?

— Does the job require some exotic material they don't normally carry?

— Does that motor have a delivery schedule longer than the entire build cycle?

— Does the job have to go out for quotes? (Add one week?)

Obviously some of these questions are rhetorical, bordering on sarcastic. But they should make a point—again, based on a lot of experience.

3   Test, 3 months

— Do you have the human resources committed to do the work?

— If the answer to the above is that you are doing it yourself, what else is on your plate? Will *it* get done?

— Will you need specialized support equipment or facilities, and are they committed to you?

— Will you have a test plan ready then, or will you sit gazing at this lifeless lump wondering where to begin?

— Why is there no redesign, rebuild, and retest shown on the schedule? By definition, testing implies a chance of failure.

— Who or what—further down the line—gets hurt if your gizmo fails the test or is otherwise delayed?

Well that's just for starters. (I'm saying that to head off a possible rating of average from the real planners out there.) But I hope it has at least begun to illustrate the skills needed and the pitfalls that exist in planning. And I hope you weren't too tired when you got to the very last question. Please, go back and take a look, because that one sneaked in probably one of the most profound issues in planning: the effect of one person's or one group's actions on the other persons or groups. In relatively large projects, it becomes absolutely necessary to maintain awareness of the effects each action has on the many other activities involved. A few pages further on in this chapter, you will find another version of the plan I just took apart. It illustrates a much more comprehensive and responsive rendering of the same plan, while still using the basic GANTT-type of approach.

GANTT-type plans may be inadequate to capture all the complex interactions of very large projects. In such cases, the *critical-path* approach is probably called for. One example of this is the *PERT network*—often referred to as the *bubble chart,* because its original hand-drawn forms invariably feature a series of interrelated circles (bubbles) containing key events in the plan. This type of planning is definitely beyond the scope of this book, though later in this chapter you will find a very simplified PERT plan covering one small part of the GANTT-type plan I have been discussing.

I do want to make two major points about PERT or critical-path analysis plans. First, when accurately laid out and regularly updated, they work beautifully; as soon as an update is completed, its effect on the whole plan, all the way to the very last event, falls out automatically. (Such an effect is seen in the illustration at the end of the chapter.) Second, they don't lend themselves to amateur production and are best handled by a professional planner. While I say this mainly because I believe that planners have the special skills and training needed for such analysis, I think that they are also sufficiently outside that project to be objective. Simply put, the planner will tell it like it is, which, however painful, is really what you want.

There are software packages out there, ranging in cost from thirty dollars to several thousand, which purport to improve your ability to make plans. I've read up on them, talked to people about them, tried several of them, and come to the conclusion that they are painful to use, are very time-consuming, and don't quite do what I or most occasional users want them to do. However, I wouldn't question their potential merit in the hands of a full-time professional planner. For those of us who make plans like the GANTT chart above, but who can't draw straight lines or print legibly, there is a neat little software package called Quick Schedule®*, which is easy to use and helpful in laying out relatively simple plans.

---

*Quick Schedule® is a registered trademark of Channelmark Corporation.

Of course, making the plan is only the beginning. You must review it frequently to see how you are doing. Having professional planners is a great advantage here also: they ensure the plan is the living thing it needs to be. Planners come around like death and taxes—and are sometimes about as welcome; but, bless their hearts, they are our conscience, and they do a lot to keep us on course. (In case you are wondering, I am not in the planning business—or the blessing business for that matter.)

I must make an important point here. The initial draft of any plan should be made by the person who is to carry it out. This person usually is the only one with the depth of knowledge necessary to draft the plan. The planner's primary role at this point is to ensure consistency and uniformity of approach and to ensure that each subplan is compatible with all others in support of the overall plan.

With or without planners, you must keep up your plan. If all is going well, it's very rewarding to see it played out. If it doesn't go well, you give yourself the maximum chance to do something about it; and that is vital!

I can't cover all the kinds of plans for all the different jobs out there, and of course, the example in this chapter relates to a particular kind of operation; more importantly, I hope I have presented a philosophy that convinces you of the importance of planning and working with the plan. But here are a few examples of other tasks that could be laid out in GANNT-type chart.

Start a new training program

— Select potential trainers.

— Have introductory meeting.

— Develop objectives (see earlier chapter on the customer concept).

— Set assignments.

— Meet for review of assignments.

— Finalize the package.

— Schedule trainees.

— Start program.

Improve loading-dock facility

— Schedule meeting with loaders.

— Develop objectives.

— Divide up and start the fact-finding.

— Meet to review results.

— Draft a proposal.

— Review it with loaders.

— Revise it.

— Have final review.

— Present to next layer of management for approval.

Don't underestimate the number of steps needed to get something done. The more detailed your plan, the more likely you are to have properly described and understood what is entailed in getting from where you are to where you need to be. If you and your people feel a great deal of uncertainty, a plan is *the best way to reduce uncertainty*. Only by setting down the steps can you begin to turn something vague into something tangible. But, like making the best decision (discussed in chapter 7), you are only expected to give it your best shot.

Following are two more ways of looking at the simple one-line schedule I used earlier in this chapter. The first type is also known as a GANTT chart. You will see that it is much more complete than the simple version you saw earlier and that it attempts to anticipate many of the potential contingencies raised in my critique of the simple plan. It only took a few minutes longer to create, but the gains might be measured in weeks or even months.

GANTT CHART TYPE OF SCHEDULE

Design plan available	x				
Other dept.'s input available	x				
Designer A available	x				
Design	x————x				
Designer B available		x			
Long lead parts ordered	x				
Quote for build requested		x (Using prelim. DRGs)			
Build		x———x			
Technician available		x			
Prepare test plan		x x			
Instruments available		x			
Electrical support needed/available		x———x			
Debug		x—x			
Test			x———x		
Analyze results				x—x	
Report results				x	
Redesign/modify				x—	

On the following pages, I illustrate the PERT network approach for the same schedule. However, for those who have never seen one before, following are some qualifications:

1 I have avoided most of the jargon that normally goes along with this type of plan; I have used complete word descriptions in places to reduce possible confusion.

(continues on page 93)

SIMPLIFIED "PERT" NETWORK FOR EARLY
STAGES OF PREVIOUS "GANTT" CHART ILLUSTRATION

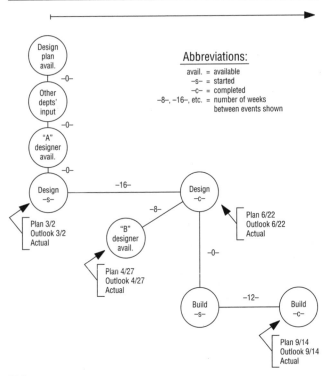

Abbreviations:

avail. = available
–s– = started
–c– = completed
–8–, –16–, etc. = number of weeks
between events shown

Notes

1 This is the plan at the outset. As indicated under "Design –s–" (design start), the *"plan,"* is to start March 2. And, at this time, the *"outlook"* is that it will also happen then. *"Actual"* will not be noted until the start does actually happen.

2 Best estimates of various activities (e.g., 16 weeks design) automatically result in "–c–" (completion) dates. A time of "–0–" (zero) weeks implies simultaneous events.

OK so far. Now let's move to the next depiction of the diagram to see what might happen.

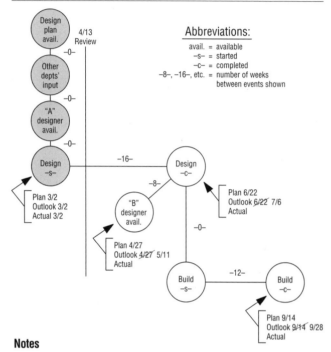

Notes

1 All four initial events took place as planned. The "actual" date has been added, and for further clarity, when completed, the events are hatched out.

2 On the sixth weekly review of 4/13, it is learned that designer "B" will be two weeks late starting. Thus the "outlook" is now 5/11.

3 Your planner dispassionately points out the domino effect so visible in this type of plan (i.e., two weeks "slip" flows through "design –c–" and on to "build –c–," now outlooked for 9/28.

4 Action required! On to the next diagram.

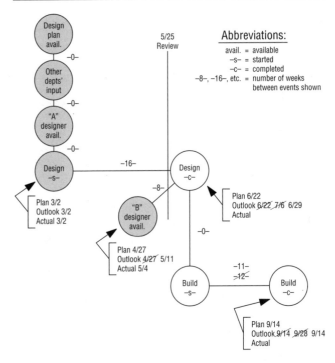

Abbreviations:

avail. = available
−s− = started
−c− = completed
−8−, −16−, etc. = number of weeks between events shown

Notes

1 We are now at the 5/25 review.

2 Through negotiation, the "B" designer was brought on only one week late instead of two. Thus, the "actual" became 5/4.

3 This moved "Design −c−" up one week to 6/29 but still left an overall lateness of one week carrying through to build completion.

4 By commiting to release many already existing drawings, design reached agreement with the workshop to reduce their time from 12 weeks to 11 weeks. Thus, the build completion outlook reverted back to the original 9/14.

2 I have only dealt with a portion of the previous GANTT type of plan—also to reduce the potential for confusion.

3 I have shown the plan as it might appear at three points in time: (a) immediately after plan completion, (b) after a review several weeks later, and (c) after another review several weeks later than that. But note that in practice, such a plan would quite properly be reviewed every week.

4 I have crossed out certain numbers but left them in place for clarity in explanation. Many professional planners would erase these numbers, but an accompanying written report would record the trail of events and changes.

After reviewing the relatively simple PERT plans shown here, I am sure many readers will agree with my earlier statement that they are not for amateurs and that the skills of a professional planner are desirable. Armed with a tool such as this, such planners can objectively show the multiple effects that result from just one event slip. This objectivity will sometimes lead to furious debates between a purely logical planner and an overly optimistic manager. I still remember with a smile being present when, after such a debate had raged for some time, the frustrated manager observed that the net effect of his slip on the program (which still had three years to run) was that the New York product announcement would be made at 11:00 A.M. instead of 10 A.M.! Seriously, my advice is the old cliché: Don't shoot the messenger.

I should add that planners usually have several versions of the PERT network with varying degrees of detail. The least-cluttered version is usually provided to the highest level of management and will illustrate only very major milestones—particularly the key completion dates or if you like, the graphic version of the bottom line.

In summarizing, I would first like to observe that of the many general management courses I have attended, none has ever dealt adequately, if at all, with the pragmatic aspects of planning as I have presented them in this chapter. I once thought that, perhaps, I was unlucky in my choice of courses, but particularly in my recent years as a consultant to a variety of companies, I have had ample evidence that education in this vitally important area is lacking. While plans usually exist, they are often so inadequate or so infrequently reviewed that the groups involved have little control over their progress.

Undoubtedly, except in a totally routine environment, a manager must acquire planning skills and ensure that his or her people acquire them also. Consistency in planning approaches is a must. After all, plans are not just meant to keep one's own group of people on course but also, by appropriate communication, to keep all other interdependent groups informed.

Finally, in a complex program environment, I strongly recommend the services of experienced planners. They can make individual plans consistent, integrate all the diverse activities, and report on progress—not just of individual groups but of the whole undertaking. It surely is worth comparing the salary of such individuals with the cost of potentially avoidable schedule slips.

10

Problem Solving

Real-life story: A person I knew through somebody else was preparing something at the kitchen sink when the smoke alarm went off. This person, following a familiar routine, got a chair and climbed up on it to remove the battery. Still reaching for the battery, the person suddenly noticed flames leaping from the stove top.

The story illustrates the first order of problem solving: understanding the real problem. I am glad the story came along when it did—partly because it saved me from having to dig into some of the same kinds of things I've done myself, and partly because I don't think I had anything quite so potentially exciting in my collection.

Paragraph three: and here's the point again. The first and possibly most important step is to define the real problem—not the symptom of the problem but the root problem. And when you think you've done that, look again; make sure it's not another symptom. And make sure there isn't more than one problem. Example, read from left to right:

Problem Symptom	Possible Causes	Possible Causes of the Causes!	and so on ...
	Dealers not stocking it	Poor dealer support	
		Poor reliability	
Widget not selling	Lack of advertisements	Lack of advertising strategy	?
	Reports of poor reliability	Build costs too high	
		Margins too high	
	Expensive relative to competitor		

This is a relatively simple overview of a problem just to illustrate the point; the actual search for a problem cause would not likely be that simple given the topic.

The longer a problem has existed, the more likely it is that its roots are widespread, and the more likely it is that a considerable effort will be required to understand all the potential causes. In effect, a complete overhaul may be required. All too often, without a rigorous examination of potential causes for the problem, an incomplete or even useless solution is developed. Most of us have experienced these partial or useless "solutions"—like the new spark plugs that didn't improve car performance because the wires were old and shorting and the carburetor needed an overhaul, or like the new brand of coffee that didn't make the brew any less bitter because the real problem was a buildup of residues in the coffeemaker.

Partial solutions also abound on grander scales: like the fast-food chain that keeps coming up with new menus to improve its market share without noting their competitor's success is partially based on their dependably clean premises and their consistently polite and cheerful staff.

Another example comes from the domestic automobile industry. A few years ago, the Big Three correctly concluded that reliability was an issue affecting their ability to compete with the imports, even though not all imports were shining examples of reliability. However, one company seemed to perceive that tastes in external styling were changing also, and they produced a more Euro-styled automobile. While it was no more reliable than any other domestic vehicle, it was a great success. I believe they succeeded because, when they examined their problem of falling sales, they widened their scope of probable root causes (that is, although they correctly perceived reliability as one cause, they also noted that people's tastes in automobile appearance were changing). Now, years later, with gains made in reliability, a study of a problem in sales compared to another company is even more likely to show a shift toward the importance of aesthetic design. As with my friend and the smoke detector, root causes for a problem can change.

I already illustrated a simple way to look at a problem earlier in this chapter. Most methods of solving problems start with a study of effects (or symptoms) and their causes. For each effect, there will be at least one cause; but each cause may, in turn, be an effect with its own causes. Experienced systematic problem solvers will have no problem with that seemingly twisted piece of logic, but let me illustrate with an example.

Your car won't start; we'll call that an *effect*. When you turn the key, you don't hear the engine turning over, and you conclude that a possible *cause* is that the starter motor has failed to operate. Now let's rename this failure of the starter motor operation an *effect*. A possible *cause* for this effect is that the battery is dead. OK? I hope that illustrates the changing roles of causes and effects. Now let's look back at it again—with the car not starting as an *effect;* and let's look at the first possible *cause*—failure of the starter motor to operate. It's also possible that the ignition switch has failed, or a wire between the switch and the motor has become disconnected, or .... And any of these possible causes may in turn become an effect. The cause for a disconnected wire may be that it is hit by the steering mechanism. I have hopefully convinced you by now that some systematic approach is needed, even for a problem as simple as this one seemed to be at the beginning. Fortunately for us, several approaches exist, and I'm going to show an application of one that is often called—surprise!—the cause-and-effect diagram.

When I wrote this book, I had no experience in the subject matter of the following problem. Yet you will notice that my cause and effect, or fishbone, diagrams, while probably incomplete in the eyes of a person experienced in the field, are nevertheless quite prolific in identifying potential causes. This is not so much a testimony to my brilliance and versatility as it is an endorsement of this systematic approach. However, drawing on the thoughts of people who are experienced in a particular field is a powerful tool for (a) understanding the factors involved and (b) providing a happy hunting ground in which one can spot potential problem areas. Just the dialogue that accompanies the development of such a diagram in a group setting may be the most important gain in the whole exercise. People in the group see, perhaps for the first time, the complete picture, with not only their part spelled out but also that of their partners.

THE PROBLEM: FALLING PROFITS OF A SMALL LOCAL THEATER
CAUSE-AND-EFFECT DIAGRAM: OVERVIEW

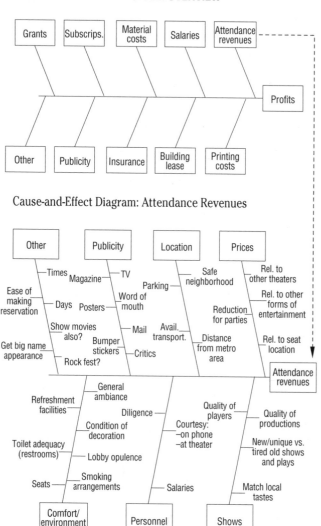

Cause-and-Effect Diagram: Attendance Revenues

Notice I split the analysis into two stages; otherwise it would have been totally overwhelming (and you thought it was overwhelming anyway?). The idea is fairly self-explanatory. Using the fishbone analogy, you put all the possible causes on the bones, which eventually connect to the head, where the effect is ultimately felt. You'll notice that some items are truly factors for consideration whereas others are almost rhetorical in that they already imply the solution. Don't get too hung up in semantics. Treat this as a brainstorming session; the important thing is to draw all the thoughts out. Again, this begs to be done with the group of people who are personally involved in the project. But it doesn't hurt to bring in an outside person or two. Outsiders are less likely to be confined by traditional thinking on the topic.

Notice also that the major "bones" are, in effect, categories that help to organize the thinking. Often, these categories break down into people-related things (for example, operator's effect on a process), equipment, and materials.

Try one on your own. They are more fun than you might think. Perhaps your spaghetti is not getting good reviews lately. Take a look at the problem as one person did in the cause-effect diagram on next page.

Whether it's a problem with spaghetti or with falling theater revenues, by completing this kind of exercise, you will have given yourself an excellent start on solving the problem. You and your people will recognize the full scope of the problem and be properly prepared to work on a solution. Indeed, potential remedial actions may already be apparent, solely due to the rigor with which this approach searches out factors that affect the outcome. At a minimum, you will almost certainly uncover the problem area or, more likely, several problem areas in the diagram you and your people have developed.

THE PROBLEM: FALLOFF IN SPAGHETTI RATINGS

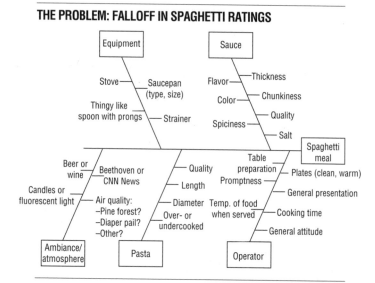

You may perceive this process as both overwhelming and a lot of work, but without it, you may be shooting in the dark. Finding out later that your solution didn't address the real problem can be much more overwhelming, not to mention at least double the work and schedule pressure.

Assuming the solution hasn't jumped out at you along with the problem, you are now faced with developing those solutions. If you have several problems, this would be the time to break into smaller problem-solving groups—probably in accordance with the major bones of the diagram.

Although the process of problem solving may be long and agonizing, the approach is not that mysterious. Most problems involve more people than just yourself, and that implies a group effort that you will lead. The important aspects of these sessions are as follows:

1 Review the problem to be sure of complete and universal understanding. Go back into the "bones" of the problem.

2 Develop *several* solutions. There is rarely only one solution. Go along in a brainstorming mode (that is, no idea is judged at this point; just get them all out and list them where everyone can see them).

3 Use the techniques discussed in the chapter on decision making to sort through the contending ideas and arrive at the best solution based on the facts available. If you are not comfortable that all the relevant facts are available, adjourn to allow the facts to be gathered. If the number of solutions offered is very large, you may want to do a simple voting exercise to reduce them to a manageable number. Enumerate the ideas, and ask each person to rate (on a piece of paper) each one on a scale of one to ten (ten being best). Then collect the results in a way that everyone can see, total them, and look for the solutions that have the greatest level of support. Warning! Make sure the voters know the subject and are, therefore, qualified to vote. Also, use your own judgment to retain an idea that doesn't receive popular support but that you nevertheless feel has merit. Sometimes one has to help democracy along with a little tweak!

4 Set some mechanism in place to follow through the implementation and to observe the results. If it doesn't pan out as expected, go back to the beginning: that is, define the problem. In many large projects with which I have been associated, there existed a *Problem Management System,* which did just what its name suggests. Now I belong to a growing school that believes that if you manage the problems, you substantially increase your chances of having a successful project. So often, I have seen projects suddenly founder because a previously identified problem was not kept visible, was forgotten, or fell through the cracks. This is quite predictable, so it makes sense to manage the problems. It's basically a simple discipline: as problems are identified, list them, publish them, and review them periodically until they are fixed!

Managing problems can promote continuous improvement by *preventing* problems—something equally important as *solving* problems. In one large program, we even listed things we hadn't started yet as problems; that way, things-not-started didn't *become* problems just due to lack of attention.

In summary, I realize that problem solving is one of the most difficult aspects of a manager's life, and I could go on for many more pages to explore the finer aspects. But it would likely be more overwhelming than helpful because no matter how much more detail is provided, how many more methods are shown, the basic approach is still this: (1) understand the problem, (2) look at several potential solutions, (3) choose the best one, and (4) follow up to see what happens.

Footnote: The foregoing has emphasized the need and the reasons for involving your people in developing the solution to a problem; never underestimate how important it is that your people accept and support a jointly arrived at solution.

Another footnote: I do like the story about the janitor who was asked why he seemed fed up. He replied that he was having a terrible day; twice the head of his broom had come off—and now the handle had come off! You must admit, he had fully subscribed to the idea of examining all possible root causes of his problem. Hopefully, he found one solution!

11

Interviewing

First, a little exercise for you, the reader:

You are near the end of interviewing someone and have realized that you want this person for the job. You now need to give this person a complete and interesting description of the position, your own operation, and if applicable, the larger organization or company that you are a part of. Go ahead; think about what you will say . . .

————

Well, how did you do? Were you ready? If you had been the interviewee, would you be feeling you really wanted this job?

Lesson: You have to be ready. You have to be prepared to compete with others for the most desirable candidates.

Preparation is important. You must have a quiet place for the interview, where you will not be interrupted; if you don't have a closed office, use a conference room or someone else's office. (While this may seem obvious to most, I recently talked to a professional person who was interviewed in a busy open office area!) Be sure that you are available on schedule or that someone else meets the candidate if you should be detained. Be sure that if someone else is to interview the candidate, that person is similarly prepared. These and similar preparations are important; the candidate has gone to some trouble to be on time, to dress appropriately, and to be prepared. The least you can do is to do the same. After all, you represent the organization. It's very difficult to make small talk to keep things going when the candidate surely knows that you have not prepared; you might as well get out the old hat and cane because you are going to have to dance for a while.

All of this might seem like common sense to most; yet I frequently get feedback about interview arrangements that fall woefully short in these areas, when in my opinion, most of them are a matter of common courtesy. I once escorted a candidate to the next interviewing manager's office only to find the manager had taken the day off without making alternative arrangements; you only do that once!

It is quite common, especially when several people are to interview a candidate, that one or more managers take the candidate to lunch. In that case, I recommend against in-depth interviewing at the meal table. Most people can't enjoy their meal under such stressful conditions. And what is the point of taking someone out to lunch and not letting them enjoy it? This is the time for discussion about hobbies, recreation, and hometown—topics that reveal other important aspects of character that together make up a complete person.

Consider the posibility that the applicant is more experienced in the interview situation than you are. This is quite probable in your early days as manager. Some students emerging from college have been prepared by their colleges as if they were the president preparing for a press conference: they already have a list of the questions you are going to ask! So you can't afford to be low on preparation.

One aspect of preparation, of course, is a study of the résumé (I'm assuming that it was good enough to lead to an interview). Look for what are known as red flags. You know the red flags for your particular profession, but there are some general ones. Check the dates of previous jobs; look for any lack of continuity. This is not necessarily bad, but it should be probed in the interview. Look at academic background; is it way over what's needed for this job? Has the applicant changed jobs with abnormal frequency in a given time? If you're interviewing a new graduate, do you see signs of jobs or other attempts to contribute to the education costs? None of these are discriminators in themselves, but if they appear to deviate significantly from the norm, you will need to gain further understanding during the interview.

The résumé or initial application may contain references; if not, you may want to ask for them during the interview.

When you first encounter your candidate, do what you can to put the person at ease; some small talk is OK, but don't overdo it—it's better to get on with the business at hand.

Particularly if you are male and the candidate is female, do not comment on the candidate's physical attractiveness or the way she dresses. Such remarks constitute a form of discrimination and harassment in the interview situation. If I once thought I would not have to write this in a book on management, recent well-publicized events have changed my position.

Unless you are unusually fluent at the interviewing business, have a cue card by you that lists the key questions you want to ask. Some people may get bent out of shape at this suggestion, but I see nothing wrong with it. I may have two hours or I may have only twenty minutes in which to understand this person enough to make a decision that will significantly affect both our lives; therefore, I want to be as thorough and consistent as I can in interviewing this and other candidates. In case some of you are imagining that I have a two-by-four-foot poster board on the wall behind the candidate, let me assure you I'm thinking of a small piece of notepaper on the desk, or even notes on the person's résumé; in the unlikely event that the candidate expresses discomfort with the notes, just explain it the way it is: that you had certain things you wanted to be sure you asked. However, don't have a form from which you bark out questions and write down the answers—that's just an application process, not an interview.

I also make notes during an interview, and this, too, is controversial; some feel it's unprofessional and impolite. I don't—unless, of course, the interviewer writes down everything. Most interviewees see it as a positive thing when the interviewer occasionally writes something down. But be judicious; if, for instance, the candidate confesses to something like a minor traffic violation, don't crash down on your desk and begin writing furiously. In the unlikely event that it matters, hold it in memory for later.

OK, now what about some questions for your cue card? Again, only you know what is important in your profession, but I would suggest some general guidelines. As I said before, your candidate may be very experienced at interviewing—perhaps more experienced than you are. And the candidate has probably rehearsed the answers to your questions!

So how will you get some authentic and spontaneous response from the candidate? First, be sure to at least cover those aspects of the candidate that appear on your evaluation form. There's nothing worse than trying to complete the form after the candidate has left and then realizing you didn't ask about a key aspect required by the form. Most companies will have a standard form for this; I give an example at the end of this chapter.

One of the keys, though, is to ask a lot of questions that can't be answered with just yes or no. "Tell me about ...." is often a good way to ask—especially if you just got a yes or no when you wanted more. Here are some other questions that tend to draw a person out.

Ask the person to describe his or her most significant accomplishment. This one can help you understand what the candidate considers to be a significant undertaking and how he or she went about it. The candidate may volunteer a very personal experience. If he or she does, it's OK to discuss the general topic, but consider the deeper personal aspects off-limits to you. Then, gently steer the person to answer the same question again—this time by relating something less personal such as a school project, a work project, and so on.

Ask the person to describe a significant problem he or she faced and solved. Be prepared to prompt (for example, problems with a car, a school subject, a bank, on the job, with another person, or with household chores). Don't forget, the person may be nervous, and while you need to probe, you should also be prepared to help this nervous person put his or her best foot forward.

Ask the person for an example of something he or she thought was done well or done poorly. Then find out why the candidate thought that way about it.

At the end of this chapter, I'll list other questions you might ask, but I hope you have the basic idea: you need to ask questions that will draw the person out and reveal something about his or her thinking. Encourage the person to give an answer that adequately demonstrates his or her abilities; a yes or no doesn't do that. While this method can expose those lacking in understanding, it equally well encourages others to demonstrate their competence. But be sure to ask similar questions of each candidate to ensure an equitable judgment process.

Now let's deal with some other kinds of questions—*those you should not ask.* Here are some examples:

1 Any questions about race, age, or religious affiliations; since these should not have any effect on the person's opportunity to fill the position.

2 Questions that might be considered overly personal, such as, "Do you intend to have a family?" "Are you a single parent?"

3 Questions that might pry into someone's socioeconomic status, such as, "Do you own a car?" "Do you have a telephone?" You would only need to know about such things if the job specifically requires them.

While most people are well aware of (1) and (2) above, I have found that some are puzzled by (3). The fact is that unless the position was described as requiring such items as a car or a telephone, such questions are of a personal nature (for example, if you are hiring a payroll clerk, it should not concern you that the person does not have a phone and will ride to work with a friend). If, on the other hand, you are hiring a realtor, and when you advertised the position you stated "must have a suitable car," then it is permissible. A general guideline to follow is this: You are only entitled to ask questions directly relating to whether or not the person has, or can acquire within the work environment, those skills required by the position.

I have not provided a complete list of questions to be avoided; the topic itself is worthy of a small book. However, it's very important that you be up-to-date on this subject and if you have any doubts, contact your personnel department or your local Equal Employment Opportunity Commission for advice; or have a human resources consultant help you. I must repeat: *This is not a complete list.*

When you have completed your questions, give the candidate an overview of the operation. Then, give the candidate the opportunity to ask you some questions. Candidates may, of course, ask questions throughout, but you will have to control the extent to which this happens or the interview may get off track, or worst case, the candidate takes control. If you perceive this happening, politely point out that your overview at the end may well cover many potential questions and that the candidate will have ample opportunity then to ask anything not covered. Justifiably, you really don't want the candidate forming an incomplete perception of the position early on in the interview and then subconsciously or otherwise answer your questions in accordance with that perception.

By this time you have probably formed a preliminary go/no-go view of the candidate, and if it's a go, you want him or her to understand the attractiveness of the job and the organization—which, I admit, is weasel-wording for the act of *selling* the job. But if the candidate is good, you are likely to have competition, and you need to put your job in its best light—without, of course, promising anything you can't deliver.

Conclude the interview politely, and assure the candidate you will get back to him or her regardless of outcome within a specified time—preferably no more than two weeks.

As soon as the candidate has left, fill out an evaluation sheet while things are still fresh in your mind. Leaving it until later may be tempting but, unless you have an unusually retentive mind, any significant delay will compromise accuracy.

Follow up on references if appropriate. Be sure to find out in what capacity the reference person knew or knows the candidate. Close friends, uncles, and aunts may have difficulty being objective; try to get previous employers (obviously not the current one), teachers, or other people who are more likely to be objective. As well as the obvious questions about reliability, punctuality, productivity, and so on, describe the potential position to the reference person and ask her or him to comment on the candidate's ability to fill it; Ask, too, about the strengths and possible shortcomings.

Now for your interview checklist:

Preparation

1 Be ready with a comprehensive description of the position and, where appropriate, of the whole organization. (As discussed in the text, hold the comprehensive job description until you have asked most or all of your questions.)

2 Review the résumé and note the red flags for later questioning.

3 Have a basic set of questions prepared for all candidates. Be sure you have questions that will give you the information needed on any standard evaluation form you may customarily use.

4 On the day of the interview, make sure someone receives the candidate on time and that any other interviewers are present and prepared.

5 Hold the interview in a quiet area where you will not be interrupted.

The interview

1 Help the candidate to be as relaxed as possible, but don't prolong the preamble.

2 Use open-ended questions; if you do, and you still get short measure, try "tell me more about...."

3 Make limited notes if something is too important to trust to memory.

4 When you have satisfied yourself with questions, provide a full description of the position and whatever larger organization applies.

5 Invite the candidate to ask questions.

After the interview

1 Complete an evaluation as soon as possible.

2 Make reference checks if appropriate.

3 Follow up with the candidate regarding the outcome—usually by mail. Be sure to thank the candidate for the interest shown, and in the event of a rejection, don't recount the reasons. Simply state that another candidate was chosen, if such was the case.

In summary, be sure that you and any others involved are well prepared. Plan your interview well ahead of time to ensure you get as much as you can in a limited time. Draw the candidate out; be sure your questions are designed to elicit more than a series of yes and no answers. Be consistent with questions, especially when you are interviewing several people for the same position. Follow up in an expedient way after the interview.

As with any kind of decision making, you can't be expected to be right every time—perhaps especially so in this case, where literally, you have a limited time for information gathering and you must make a decision that may affect the candidate and your organization for years to come. Again, you can only be expected to make your best decision. But it will certainly help if you are properly prepared and if you structure your questions consistently so that you can make fair comparisons.

Here is the list of interview questions I promised earlier.

— What are your long- and short-range objectives? (Most college grads expect you to ask this one!)

— What is it about the position that particularly grabbed your interest?

— What kinds of things have you done that we should be particularly interested in?

— What didn't I ask you that you wish I had asked?

— How would you go about (pose a problem that should be well within the person's abilities and look for methodical approach, ability to reason, inventiveness, and so on)?

— What kinds of things don't you like to do?

— Tell me about a (product, organization, person, and so on) you admire and why.

— Tell me about a (product, organization, and so on)

you feel could be improved and what you would do to improve it.

— What has been your most significant accomplishment? Tell me why it was so significant.

— Which of your personal strengths do you think should be attractive to this company?

— What would be the ideal job for you? Why?

— Why do you want to leave your current situation?

— What was your most disappointing experience in your current situation? What might you have done to improve the situation?

— What might you have done to obtain a higher grade in college?

— What has been your best job so far? Why?

— What would constitute excessive pressure for you in the workplace?

— Are you willing to travel? Relocate? (Ask this only if it is a job requirement.)

— Have you ever just taken a thing or a situation and improved it? Tell me about it.

— Have you ever been in a situation where you have had to take charge or provide a lead for others? Tell me about it.

Some of these questions clearly overlap. My intent is simply to suggest the kinds of questions likely to elicit more than a one-line answer, or worse yet, a yes or no.

Following is an example of an evaluation form to be completed soon after the candidate leaves. The simulated data in the form relate to an accounting position and are completely fictitious, as I am sure an accountant could quickly point out. Note that although the form might apply to a person currently in the working community, you can also use it effectively with new college graduates. Some of the sample comments are inspired by my extensive experience in hiring new graduates; one of the most rewarding experiences is to find graduates who have done so much more than just go to school and, consequently, warrant entries in all the boxes.

CANDIDATE EVALUATION FORM

Name: A. N. Other   **Degree:** A.A.S. Accounting

Position being considered: Accountant III   **Interviewed by: / Date:** *J. B. Jones 3/3*

Description	Exc.	VG	G	Fair	Poor	Comments
Education: Appropriateness of choice, level of achievement		✓				Education clearly fits career choice. GPA 3.5
Work Achievement: Evidence of successful application, growth		✓				In school currently but has evening job doing accounts for several local stores
Initiative: Evidence of self-motivation, leadership	✓					Heads up student financial assistance program
Ability to Reason: Logical thought process, ability to think through a problem	✓					When presented with our "xxx" problem, came up with our current solution!
Personality: Conversational skills, smartness of attire, general personality, etc.	✓					Very easy to talk with. Mature thought process. Very neatly dressed. Slightly reserved, good sense of humor. Confident.
Overall:	✓					Clearly exceptional

Other: Speaks French fluently. Earns free trips to France as assistant guide.

Summary Remarks: Excellent candidate for our training program, especially international division.

12

Performance Appraisal

Each employee should receive a formal performance appraisal at least once a year; it should be a requirement and a carefully scheduled event. This is usually a basis for a salary increase at that time or later. Now, most of you are probably thinking that's fairly fundamental, but when I was asked to review the operations of a department in an (externally) well-respected organization not too long ago, I was unpleasantly surprised to find no such routine in place. In talking to the employees, I found they were displeased about the lack of a formal process and mystified about the derivation of their annual increases and their standing in the organization.

Performance appraisals have some things in common with filing your income tax return; the forms are a pain to complete, take a lot of time to do properly, and sometimes precipitate a stressful encounter. No wonder people like to avoid doing them. And yet, in any normal organization of appreciable size, it is unacceptable to operate without a regularly scheduled performance appraisal process in place. Management is clearly obliged to provide one to each employee. A regular performance review gives people a clear idea of where they stand relative to what you expect of them and where they are headed.

The process should occur at least once a year—probably more often in the case of a new hire. Even for established people, an appraisal once a year potentially leaves a long gap in communication on this most important topic, so I strongly recommend at least one scheduled meeting in between annual reviews to discuss the same kinds of things without necessarily putting a rating on performance. One of the main purposes of such meetings should be what I refer to as on-course correction—making sure the employee is on the best course for a good annual review, clearing up any misunderstandings about what is expected, and if necessary, correcting the present course.

The employee should not be substantially surprised at the content of a formal review. Indeed, if the employee is genuinely and substantially surprised by negative content in an annual review, you have probably messed up. Note the word *substantially;* I'm not talking about a nit that excusably escaped your notice. I'm talking about large gaps in understanding of expectations that you should have dealt with along the way. It is simply not acceptable to wait until performance-appraisal time to deal with a performance shortfall. It is, of course, acceptable to record poor performance in a performance appraisal when you have made every effort to apply on-course corrections.

What form should the paperwork take? I initially thought that a large company I worked for had a very good format for the technical (all nonclerical) staff, until it eventually dawned on me that the secretaries and certain other clerical staff had a much better one.

The technical people's format was the fairly familiar "two-sider" arrangement. On one side, the employee writes what he or she did; on the other side, the manager writes how well it was done and usually rates each item on a scale such as 1 to 5 with 1 being poor and 5 being outstanding. Advantages of this approach are that the employee has the opportunity to record all she or he did in the preceding months and that the manager gets an accounting so that memory (or lack of it) is not a factor in fully evaluating each individual's activities. This format is, of course, particularly suited to a situation where the work load can be broken into specific tasks.

The secretaries' format was similar, but it also had another sheet on which the manager was required to check a box to indicate how well the secretary performed against specific performance attributes. Nursing organizations seem to use a similar approach.

Why this format only applied to the secretaries at that company escapes me because it seems considerably more objective than the other kind I described. One problem I saw with sole use of the two-sider approach for the technical people was that so much depended on the literary talents of the people involved; indeed, reading some of them (including some of my own earlier masterpieces) is apt to raise a smile because of the obvious pains the writer has gone to in order to achieve a memorable piece of prose.

The specific-performance-attribute form is really quite concise and easy to complete. Moreover, it ensures that the manager rates each employee against a consistent set of attributes. It's somewhat akin to the decision-making process introduced in chapter 7, where we arrayed choices against the same set of attributes. By itself, this format is well suited to situations where the work load is of a routine or continuous nature (that is, it cannot be broken down into specific, separable events or tasks). However, consistent with the concerns I expressed above, I would recommend its use as a supplement to the two-sider.

OK, I've talked about the forms, and each reader has now got an idea of what they might look like. But probably, no two ideas are alike, so let me illustrate.

THE TWO SIDER

Activity	Appraisal
Testing of the new widget. Built the test fixture, wrote a test plan, and conducted the test. Completed the report that summarized the results and provided recommendations for improvement.	Mary performed well on this task. Her test plan was thorough, and the test was successful. She completed the report in a timely manner and her well-considered recommendations resulted in significant improvements. Rating 3 (satisfactory)

In a technical environment, three to eight such activities might appear in a typical appraisal, and this format clearly identifies the specific activities. The appraisal in this case looks quite positive, perhaps suggesting a better than "satisfactory" performance.

At the end of the listing of individual activities, there is usually a space for the manager to enter an overall rating and overall comments (typical examples of appropriate forms are illustrated at the end of this chapter). However, a plain mathematical average of the individual ratings often will not give the correct overall rating (that is, a particularly large activity for which a 3 rating was given when combined with two very small activities rated 5 and 4 should not result in an overall rating of $(3 + 5 + 4) / 3 = 4$.

You can either make a judgment as to the overall rating or calculate using appropriate weightings for each task. In the following example using the same ratings, the manager weighted the tasks according to the amount of time they took relative to the total time period, 80 percent, 10 percent, and 10 percent, respectively. Thus, the rating formula would look like this:

$(0.8 \times 3) + (0.1 \times 5) + (0.1 \times 4) = 3.3$ (which you may reasonably round down to 3, or the not uncommon 3+)

(The use of a plus or minus sign after individual and overall scores has been a controversial subject in my experience. I am personally in favor of such additions, since I think they add important extra meanings to the ratings. In the case above, the recipient of a 3+ knows that she comfortably met the rating, even slightly exceeded it; a 3– would indicate otherwise.)

Less obvious than the method for arriving at this number is its criticality in conjunction with the overall, or general, comments. I can assure you that most managers, when reviewing in-house performance appraisals for potential additions to their group, proceed immediately to the end of the appraisal for the overall rating and general comments; some will not look any further! Thus, the rating must be as accurate as possible, and the general comments (typically a relatively brief capsule summary) must capture the key attributes of the individual concerned.

Now let's look at an appraisal format that concentrates strictly on specific attributes.

Attribute	E	VG	S	F	P	Comments
Productivity			X			Mary's output is always at or above the expected level.
Quality of work		X				VG in both actual testing and in clear reports.
Initiative			X			Mary can be relied upon to be self-starting.
Timeliness of work completion			X			Projects dependably completed on time.
Punctuality				X		Still needs to improve consistency in arriving on time in the morning.
Interpersonal skills	X					Mary goes out of her way to help others and is liked by everyone.
Attitude about organization			X			Mary is active in a quality circle.

Adding this appraisal to the preceding one, we have a more complete picture of Mary and a more objective view of her overall performance than we will have from a summation on a series of two-siders. Equally important, we can compare her in a consistent and equitable manner with others in her group because we will apply this same set of attributes to each in turn; and we have previously arrived at these attributes as being the important ones relative to the work of this group. We can see that Mary has strength in some important areas: her work quality is very good, and she has excellent relationships with others. On the other hand, she apparently is not a morning person, and this may be affecting her overall strength and future progress. Others in the group, for example, do just as good a job, and you can depend on them to be available at all times of the day. Note that some attributes get at things that can indirectly affect the group's performance. For example, a great performer in the skills area can nevertheless drag down the group if she or he is a pain in the neck to get along with or sometimes can't be found when a visitor arrives in the morning to look at the work going on.

Such performance attributes can, of course, be alluded to in the two-sided format, but it's less likely to happen in a consistent and objective manner. In addition, the availability of information in this format should add an objective measure to those annual meetings held in larger companies at which several managers within a group have to market their people's merits in order to secure appropriate pay increases for them. On the downside, this format doesn't relate to specific activities, which is why, for most situations involving discreet, separable tasks carried out over a relatively long period (typically a year), I suggest a combination of the two formats. Note that you would only need to complete one attribute-type form—not one for each task or activity. An additional example of the attribute-related format is shown at the end of this chapter.

Let's assume now that you have a satisfactory format, and you have filled it out for each of your people. My advice for most people who have reached this point is to *put the completed appraisals away somewhere for a day or two!* Then take them out again and critique them as objectively as you can. Do they sound objective, or do they tend to be fluffy? Does each assessment tend to say "good—but," so that the whole thing is a net neutral (which will come across as a net negative)? Have you been glowing in your assessment of somebody not so much because this person did a good job but because their charming nature or the accolades of others unduly influenced you? Where you have implied a deficiency, can you support it with examples? Or is it just a feeling—in which case it doesn't belong here? Does the person have a serious shortcoming that you could have—but did not—discuss prior to this time? Generally, think ahead to the discussion of this appraisal, and be sure that you have made it as fair and objective as it needs to be so that you can support it at that time.

Finally, you will present the completed appraisal to the employee. This, of course, will take place in your office or some other private place where you will not be interrupted. Set a time and a duration. I suggest only about twenty minutes, because first, you have many of these to get through, and second, you should not engage in any lengthy discussion, hassle, or whatever on this occasion (more on this later). No point in a lot of idle chatter at the beginning; you both know it's "that time again."

Once you're settled, give the person time to read the appraisal. I often tell the person I'm going to give them a few minutes on their own at this point and they should take their time. Then I leave for a few minutes so the person can read without feeling pressure to get through it fast. (Picture yourself trying to concentrate on your performance appraisal with your manager sitting there drumming his or her fingers on the desk!) After the person has had time to digest the appraisal, you resume by, of course, finding out the person's reaction to it. If the reaction is positive, don't add any new information or observations—positive or negative. This can throw a wrench in the works. You went to some trouble to get a set of facts clear for this appraisal; stick to the script—within reason of course. If the reaction is seriously negative, stick to the scheduled time for this meeting; identify the area of concern, and then set another meeting no earlier than the next day to jointly examine it. This gives you both an opportunity to calm down if need be, to examine facts, and to be as objective as possible at this next meeting.

Very often, an appraisal form contains an area in which the person who has just been appraised may respond in writing to the appraisal. If the person seems distressed with the appraisal, you should point out, in a nonthreatening way, that whatever the person writes here will live on as a permanent record, and that he or she may be uncomfortable with it in the future. You may even suggest that the person hold the appraisal for a day or two and take adequate time to consider what to record here.

The last thing to be done at this meeting is to get the employee to sign the appraisal. Usually you can complete this step even if the employee objects to the appraisal, since the wording prior to the signature usually states that the employee is only attesting to having received and read it—*not* agreeing with the content.

It used to be quite common to give the employee details of the consequent salary increase at this same meeting. More recently, some have seen fit to separate the two events. I've seen it work successfully both ways, but on balance, I'm inclined to favor separation; this helps ensure that the discussions at appraisal time are purely performance related.

With the performance appraisals completed and fed back to the employees, it's natural to heave a sigh of relief because it's over for another year; and if you've done it well, it certainly is an accomplishment you can take some pride in. In fact, you are *entitled* to a sigh of relief and a few minutes silent contemplation of your office ceiling, or whatever you usually contemplate at such times. However, it's important to regard the appraisal in its proper perspective; it's an assessment of the performance of individuals in a work group that is carried out within a common time frame following a relatively long period of work. For most individuals, it is probably the culmination of a year's endeavors. Its positive aspects are that (1) it is a discipline that you and your people mutually accept, (2) it ensures that an assessment takes place at a regular interval, (3) it helps the manager make the comparisons needed to properly apportion the funds available for pay increases, and (4) it provides both your people and the company with a track record that will help in reviewing future progress and opportunities.

But let's go back a few lines to the expression "culmination of a year's endeavors." I find that a bit awesome. If the rating came out below the person's expectations, isn't it awesome to think that his or her whole year's effort was somehow misdirected? off target? If it was at the expected level, could it have been even better? I'm leading to the fact that next year's performance-appraisal process has already begun. The fact is that an important part of your job is to provide *continuous* feedback throughout the year to each individual in your group. You might consider yourself as a coach; after all, sports teams surely do better throughout the year and in the finals if they have, as a team and individually, been receiving feedback on a regular basis. (And let's not forget who comes under fire first if the team doesn't do well!) But you can only provide ongoing performance feedback if you have established appropriate individual objectives and have stayed in touch with the objectives. The rest is a matter of awareness on your part.

(It's not my intent to go into what is an appropriate challenge, but I do have a hint from my own experience. I usually encouraged my people to slightly overload themselves; not secretly, they knew what I was doing. I would openly refer to it as the 110 percent level. Invariably, the outcome would be in excess of 110 percent accompanied by a strong sense of fulfillment and—yes—enjoyment. You will not generally find the happiest, most fulfilled people among those with only just enough, or less, to do.)

Feedback may be divided into two forms: (a) positive encouraging and (b) negative encouraging. No, that's not a typo; I do mean *negative encouraging*. You can't always give positive feedback; sometimes something is not going as well as it could, and you will need to apply what I referred to previously in this chapter as on-course correction. If you do it sensitively, it should be encouraging: the person perceives that you care enough about the outcome to provide this additional guidance. In the case where the person is unwilling to respond, and you have examined your own expectations carefully for reasonableness, then you are into something much more serious, something beyond the scope of this book; indeed, it's a subject—poor performance—worthy of a book in itself. The only one I know of and found to be quite practical is called *Analyzing Performance Problems, or You Really Oughta Wanna,* by Mager and Pipe (Fearon Publishers, Inc., Belmont, CA).

Positive feedback is generally more pleasant for both parties involved. Strangely enough, it is nevertheless sometimes neglected, and a person may go for a considerable period in some doubt as to their performance until it's finally put forth in the performance appraisal. I've slipped up in this respect more than once; so remember, even good folks need to be told they are good from time to time. Let's be honest with ourselves; don't we all enjoy a compliment? Oh, some might shrug their shoulders and say, "It was nothing." But deep inside, something glows, and more important, confidence is enhanced.

By the way, there's a jeopardy here, more particularly in the United States. Sometimes a response such as "it was nothing" can offend the person paying the compliment. It sounds like a criticism of their judgment. Much better to accept the compliment with a thank you. With people of European background, a shrug of the shoulders accompanied by "it was nothing" is more common, and the person giving the compliment should not feel offended by such a reaction.

There are other ways to give positive feedback—ranging from an encouraging word to a Caribbean cruise for the whole team. While I am not going to cover the myriad ways here, I will say that, I do not favor large prizes dangled as carrots to encourage people to do just what they are expected to do. For instance, promising a luxurious vacation if a group gets a product out on schedule seems to me to lack professionalism, since surely the people involved generally have an implicit obligation to do just that! However, following some significant accomplishment, a spontaneous celebration or award for teams or individuals can be a very appropriate gesture from an appreciative organization. (I understand the dangled carrot is a widely practiced form of incentive in sales and similar organizations, where they are, presumably, effective. I don't profess to know or understand the environment of such organizations and would like to make it clear that my lack of enthusiasm for such schemes should not be interpreted as criticism of those in whose particular environment they have proved effective.)

But the effect of one-time awards dissipates rapidly, which brings us back to day-to-day feedback and counseling as by far the most enduring and effective ways to maintain optimum personal performance—and, just as important, the dependent group performance. This requires that you stay in touch with your people and their tasks and that you let them know your impressions of their work often enough that they know if they are on course; this applies whether they are performing at, above, or below expectations.

And now, your performance-appraisal checklist:

General

1 Make the commitment to carry out formal appraisals on a schedule.

2 Make sure your appraisal format really reflects the attributes that are important to your organization. Consider combining two types, as discussed earlier in this chapter.

3 If in doubt about whether to discuss pay increases at the same time you are giving an appraisal, my advice is to award the pay increase later (see text discussion).

Preparation

1 Make sure employees understand how to complete the form(s). Make sure that in their narratives, they must be objective and state facts only, not opinions. For example, it's OK for the person being appraised to write, "My efforts resulted in a savings to the company of $30,000," assuming it's true; it's not OK for that person to write, "My efforts went particularly well."

2 Make sure your written response is equally objective. For example, it's OK to say, "This aspect of the task was extremely well done"; it's not OK to say, "It's not clear whether or not this could have been done in a more efficient manner." You'll have quite a time defending that one!

3 After you have completed your part of any appraisal, *put it away,* at least overnight. Oh, I know, it's late already; but still put it away! Then read it through again. Check for objectivity. Think about questions you will be asked and whether you will have the answers. Check again for fair comparisons and for consistency with your appraisals of others in your group—particularly if there has been a significant time lapse between completing the first and the last of these appraisals.

Presenting

1 Make sure you have a quiet place where you won't be disturbed.

2 Get right down to business; the weather is of no concern right now. Still, make sure the person feels no time pressure; he or she must have adequate time to peruse the document.

3 When you are sure the person has at least read the document in its entirety, determine the person's general reaction to it. If there are quite minor explanations required, go ahead and give them. If, however, there is obviously a major difference in perceptions, set another meeting within the next one to two working days to explore these differences thoroughly.

After the appraisal process is completed

1 Think about who might have done better and what you might be able to do about it before the next appraisal time comes around.

2 Keep on coaching!

In summary, your appraisal process must be both objective and equitable. I have suggested here a combination of two formats I am familiar with, and you will find generic examples of these at the end of this chapter. The process must occur on a regular schedule, and you should hold other one-on-one meetings with employees in between formal appraisals. The formal appraisal should not contain substantial surprises; if it does, somebody goofed, and most likely it was you. Set a time limit on the meeting to discuss the appraisal; any extended discussions should be scheduled for a later date in a much longer time slot, and both of you can use the intervening time to carefully consider all the facts. In between performance appraisals, coach!

On the following pages are examples of forms you might use in an appraisal process. There is no invention here; such forms are relatively generic and are quite commonly found in larger companies. However, my advocacy of the combination of the two, for reasons described in the text, is far less common.

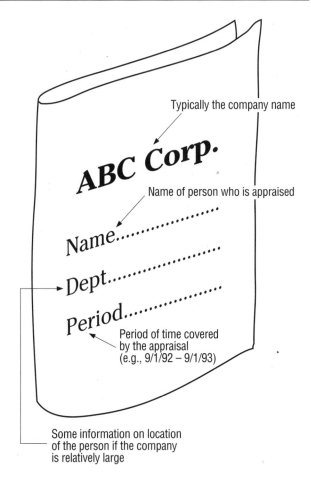

Typically the company name

ABC Corp.

Name of person who is appraised

Name....................

Dept....................

Period....................

Period of time covered
by the appraisal
(e.g., 9/1/92 – 9/1/93)

Some information on location
of the person if the company
is relatively large

Page 1, typical two-sided appraisal (usually four pages of
8½"¥ 11"size)

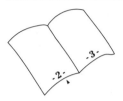

Activities	Manager's Appraisal

Pages 2 and 3 will be identical. They will both have a left-hand column in which the employee will describe his or her activities. Over a one-year period, the number of activities ranges from three to eight. On the right-hand side, the manager will comment on the activity and assign a numerical rating.

- 4 -

Overall rating for this period	
Comments by manager	

Manager's signature: Date:

Next-level manager: Date:
(if required)

Comments by employee:
(optional)

Employee's signature: Date:

Explanation of ratings:

1	Poor performance	4	Exceeding expectations
2	Below expectations	5	Outstanding
3	Expected level of performance		

Page 4 is used to summarize overall performance for the period via a numerical rating (e.g., 3 might appear in the top right corner) and the manager's comments. All aspects of this and previous page illustrations are discussed in the text. Again, the example shown is generic. Your organization's specific needs will dictate your own application.

SAMPLE ATTRIBUTE-BASED PORTION OF APPRAISAL

Attributes	Ex	VG	G	Fair	Poor	Comments (optional)
Quality of work		✓				
Level of output		✓				
Initiative			✓			
Timeliness of work completion			✓			Could improve on turning in reports on time.
Inventiveness		✓				
Capacity for problem solving		✓				
Clarity of reporting				✓		Should continue efforts to improve presentation of data.
Punctuality			✓			
Getting along with other people	✓					Makes special effort to help new people settle. Liked and respected by peers.
Involvement in company improvement activities			✓			
OVERALL		✓				Continued strong technical growth. Interpersonal skills a major asset to group.

13

Documentation of Processes and Practices

As I wrote this, I could almost sense the excitement my readers would one day experience on contemplating the title of this chapter—probably about as much (or little?) as I would. If you are like me, your responses have probably run the gamut from taking a coffee break to flipping over the pages to see how long this chapter goes on; if you did the latter, you have found out that it's not long!

I'm not going to cover the myriad paperwork schemes that are used to requisition, move, or buy something. Instead, I'm going to refer to the concepts already covered in this book and strongly suggest that you formalize the ones that apply to your operation; for the fact is, in most cases, it is absolutely necessary to do so in order to (a) capture successful processes and ensure that everyone benefits from their availability and (b) ensure that everyone uses the same process and that, therefore, the outcomes can be compared, judged, or whatever on an "apples-to-apples" basis. How, for instance, could one decide whether to spend the money on Project A or Project B when the authors of Project A went through all the steps of determining customer needs, while the authors of Project B just waved their arms in the air and assumed what the customer needs were? The answer is not to award it to Project A because they did their homework; Project B might be the better one. The only way to find out is by a consistent proposal process. So let's start with that one.

First, the steps described in the chapters about customer concept and customer needs should be formalized and used by everyone, whether you're considering a new or variant product or service or whether you're reconsidering an existing one (or anytime, for that matter, if you are not sure you're currently headed in the right direction).

Second, a decision-making process is worth formalizing. I showed some approaches in chapter 7. When making a proposal, then, you can demonstrate to all concerned what path you took to your decision and what you considered and discarded. Thus, you demonstrate that you rationally considered alternatives leading to a convincing decision—convincing because of the scope of the process. But, *please,* keep it as simple as you can. Remember that those on the receiving end of the proposal have not had a fraction of the time with the proposal that you have. All too often, I have seen a group thoroughly turned off by a very competent person with an excessively detailed proposal.

Third, a meeting process can be formalized, as has been done in many of the larger companies, resulting not only in less wasted time but in greatly improved quality of meetings.

Fourth, planning *must* be done and *must* be formalized; I think I banged on this rather heavily in the planning chapter, so I'll spare you a reiteration of the reasons why.

Fifth, problem-solving approaches should be consistent. The chapter on this subject shows some ways to make them go. Solving problems culminates in decisions and, like decisions, the path taken to get there should be apparent to all concerned. Thus, you should develop a process for problem solving in your environment and everyone should adopt it.

Last, the performance-appraisal process is not practiced as universally as I would have expected; yet I think it's a must for almost any organization. In the relevant chapter, I have suggested ways for making the process more consistent, which should allow you to better compare your people with each other.

I'd like to write a final few words on the development of processes. In the past, large companies have tended to put large numbers of people on the task of developing and documenting key process elements; often these people are not experienced in the trenches of the operation for which they are doing this work. All too often, the result is an overwhelming level of documentation that, however well intended, produces as much cynicism as support from the folks that it was supposed to serve (and the key word is *serve!*). I admit that I once resisted a process change initially (a change I regard today as a most powerful one) because of the shear enormity of the documentation package. Simplicity and brevity are essential; a small group that includes a liberal proportion of end users is most likely to produce an acceptable package.

EPILOGUE

I have devoted most of this book to presenting pragmatic approaches to key management skills, applicable to a wide variety of organizations. I have also taken into account, as far as possible, varying degrees of management experience in the readers. Beginners may be faced with many new concepts to digest, whereas veterans may have benefited from alternative views of the manager's role. However, while competency in such skills is admirable in itself, something else is present when an organization of people stands out above others. I believe you will have found the clues to that something else in chapter 1, "The Oasis." For, maybe, *that* is where leadership begins.

INDEX